Avoiding Retirement Hell

Using Old School Strategies

Don Pollock CPA

Avoiding Retirement Hell - Using Old School Strategies

Copyrighted © 2018 by Don Pollock

Publisher CTP Press

London

Don can be contacted at don.retirementhell@gmail.com

First Edition

ISBN   978-0-9959105-3-9

Website   donpollock.com

Cover Design by Kelly Hunt

Old Love

There is no greater joy than when my old dog leaves her rug and limps toward me with a greeting when I return home. She lays back down and goes to sleep. It is the sweet spot of life. Her last days were the best time of my life and the worst. Sleep well my Tessa.

CONTENTS

INTRODUCTION

The sweet spot in retirement occurs when we have sufficient financial resources to live our desired lifestyle. It commences when we leave the workforce and starts to fade with the onset of health issues. If you make it to this spot, you have won the race. The wealthy have always been able to enjoy a financially secure retirement, but the floodgates opened when baby boomers started to retire. Armed with defined benefit pension plans and beautiful mortgage-free homes, they are riding into the sunset with more wealth than any previous generation. However, the gateway is closing for many families. In the next few decades, a new elite - the upper-middle class will be the primary entrants into the sweet spot of retirement. Unfortunately, for a large part of our population, retirement will be a period of too little income and a place where dreams go to die.

The number of families that are members of a pension plan continues to decline. Employment in the manufacturing sector has shrunk and jobs have moved overseas. The number of men between the age of twenty-five and fifty-five having full-time employment is at record lows while the number of seniors in the workforce is at an all-time high. Disability insurance has become a primary source of income for many families. The concept of cradle to grave employment is either dead or dying. According to labor participation statistics, less than 70% of working age adults participate in the workforce and the number falls to under 60% for white working-class males. Combine this group with those who work but have no pension and minimal savings and we are facing a retirement crisis. Families must take every step possible to ensure they do not endure a thirty-year retirement with government pensions as their primary source of income. It is very challenging for many working families to save for retirement when their income is used to fund living expenses. Paying for a home, raising children and dealing with the ongoing expenses of having a life, often puts saving for retirement on the back burner.

The increased inequality between those who can and cannot afford retirement will result in significant issues for our country. The cost to the government to provide pensions, subsidize nursing home costs and deliver the necessary health care to the flood of baby boomers hitting retirement homes will be enormous. Much of this cost will be passed on to a middle class that already feels overtaxed.

The ability to avoid retirement hell depends on an individual's current situation. A fifty-year-old unemployed factory worker, with no savings and a large mortgage, will face significant challenges in retirement. Whereas, a young woman entering her first year of college has a lifetime to achieve financial success and save for retirement. Unlike the era of her parents, success will not just happen. She needs a plan and to be lucky enough to avoid the various curve balls that life can throw her way.

One of the biggest obstacles facing many families is indifference. Too many people lack a plan for the future, rather they just let life happen. This book will lay out strategies to avoid retirement hell, but families need to determine their potential financial situation in retirement and address these issues while they are working and time is still on their side.

Three Tributaries to Retirement

Our country can be divided into three streams as we approach retirement:

The New Elite

It consists of the wealthy and those at the upper echelon of the middle class. They have the financial

2

resources to make retirement an enjoyable phase of life.

Middle Class

They have a legitimate shot at a financially secure retirement, but they live on a slippery slope. Success depends upon retaining their jobs until retirement, avoiding economic bad luck and saving sufficient money to supplement their government and private pension income.

Low-Income Minimal Pensions (LIMP)

These families have income levels that make it impossible to save for retirement. Their income will be primarily government pensions which will fund a modest lifestyle. If government pensions are their primary source of income, it will be a challenge to enjoy retirement while living in poverty. On the bright side, this group is just one major lottery win away from financial security.

My work experience has been in the areas of taxation, pensions and retirement planning. My peers who obtained a degree and worked for large companies appear to be enjoying a phenomenal retirement, yet they share a concern whether their children can be as fortunate. Most of my generation made more money than their parents, but it appears that trend is reversing. Much of our success resulted from being a member of the baby boomers who were the luckiest generation in history. We were provided with opportunities that with minimal effort could be transformed into some level of financial success.

This book paints a portrait of retirement hell and lays out various strategies that families can utilize to avoid poverty in their final years. The ideas presented are based on old-school philosophies, such as spend less money than you earn, initiate a savings plan, invest in education, purchase a home and approach life with a moral compass. It works best when family members help each other, but to some, these strategies are relics of a bygone era. We shall review the impact of ethics on retirement as appropriate behavior and strong character will maximize an individual's chances of success. A government committed to ethics and ridding society of corruption will increase our prosperity and quality of life. The key to our future is a strong middle class, but it is currently under siege. I believe with all my heart that ethics matter, but as I watch the world unfold around me, this belief is being severely challenged.

The level of poverty in retirement will become a humanitarian crisis, yet as a society, we are not addressing these challenges. To appreciate the magnitude of the problem, consider the 1/3 rule. Over 1/3 of families will be dependent upon government support to pay their bills and that period will approximate 1/3 of their life. When health care is added to the equation, our overextended government may lack the financial resources to eradicate or significantly mitigate poverty among seniors.

PART ONE

PORTRAIT OF RETIREMENT HELL

CHAPTER ONE

STARTING AT THE END

Everyone has a plan until you get hit in the mouth.
Mike Tyson

Let's start at the end. How do you picture your last moments on this earth? You may imagine yourself at home surrounded by friends and family, but all too often we are in a hospital bed in great discomfort. Tubes and medical devices are connected to our various body parts and our time may be spent wishing the end would come sooner rather than later.

Conny had just turned fifty and had achieved a level of contentment with her life. She is the office manager of a small company and although it does not provide a pension or benefits, the salary affords a modest but comfortable lifestyle. Then all hell broke loose. Her doctor had just advised that she has stage 1V pancreatic cancer. The survival rate is low and he recommended she get her affairs in order. The doctor talked about treatment options such as chemotherapy, radiation, surgery or palliative measures to relieve the pain, but Conny knew her end was near. She understood her reality as she watched a friend die of this dreadful disease a few years earlier. Her friend fought the good fight, but the suffering was intense and the outcome was inevitable. Conny knew that she would have too few tomorrows.

The drive home from the physician's office seemed to take forever. Her mind raced through a million options and the tears never stopped flowing. Once home, she grabbed a cup of coffee, turned on the computer and attempted to research various options. Conny's mindset was not to endure extreme pain to prolong the inevitable. She wanted to die peacefully surrounded by family, not in a hospital after a painful round of treatments. She did not want to burden her family either financially or emotionally. Her first thoughts were to find a miracle cure. There were advancements in cancer treatment and she explored articles on rapid gene sequencing and genetic engineering. Then she remembered a comment attributed to Steve Jobs, the founder of Apple who died of pancreatic cancer in 2011. He stated that being the richest man in the cemetery was not important to him. Perhaps his wealth and access to the world's best medical care extended his life for a short period of time, but the outcome was never in doubt.

She knew she had a short period of time left, so her focus was to initiate an exit strategy. To her surprise, she had a period of clarity as she planned her final days. She wanted to avoid the inevitable anguish that was coming her way. If she could not die at home, her options were a hospital, a palliative care facility, or arranging her own death with the help of a foreign physician. She discovered that some countries allow euthanasia or doctor-assisted suicide. She learned about a concept known as suicide tourism. People that live in areas where assisted suicide is not legal could travel to countries such as Belgium where the lethal procedure could be administered. Conny thought it was beyond cold to buy a one-way ticket to Belgium, get euthanized, be cremated and return home in someone's carry-on luggage.

A plan had to be developed, but her family was unaware of her condition and she was uncertain if their feedback would make a difference. Would she receive more pleasure traveling the world or was time better spent with her family? Her youngest daughter had a successful career and was engaged to an amazing young man.The middle child was a single mom with three of the world's most beautiful children. She cared for her grandchildren whenever possible and discovered the joy of grandparenting was more special than she had ever imagined. Her oldest child had a mental disability and had always lived with her mother. Conny has been separated for over a decade, but never finalized the divorce. This has become an issue since Conny had recently moved in with John who was a thoughtful and caring man, but he has been unemployed for over a year since the plant closed. Other than not having a job and a preference not to have pets, John was the perfect man to share her life. He tolerated Conny's dog Daisy who was a three-year-old golden lab and played the role of family princess. Then it hit her, what does she do with Daisy? She knew John does not want the dog and her girls have living arrangements that would not accommodate a large animal.

She called her daughters and invited them to the house that evening. As the meeting with her children approached, she was overcome with fear. She had many issues to face and was overwhelmed by the unfairness of the situation. If she fought the good fight to the bitter end, it could drain most of her money and she wanted to leave a modest nest egg to her children. How should she split any inheritance with her daughters? An equal split seemed fair, but one daughter was financially secure and the oldest daughter will need assistance for the rest of her life. Conny thought she would always provide the required care, but that was no longer an option. Her other daughters could not make the necessary commitment and it was too great a burden to lay on John. Her former spouse had not been in contact with his daughters for over a decade and that was probably for the best. Throughout her life, Conny was adamant that her daughter would not be put into the "system," but it was now an option that had to be considered.

Her home was debt free. If it was sold to provide an inheritance or fund her oldest daughter's lifetime care, John would have to leave his home and it was the only house her oldest daughter had ever known. She had no lawyer, no financial planner and no friends with the financial acumen to walk her through the crisis. She wanted to quit working but needed money to pay the bills. Conny had no estate plan, modest resources and despite a life well loved and well lived, her time was near. She knew she had a shelf life but never thought it would come this early. Conny did have a will, but it was out of date. It was prepared while she was married and her former spouse was still the beneficiary of her estate. Conny did not know if the will was still valid since she has been separated for over ten years, but that was just another item to put on her to-do list.

Conny had thought she would inherit money in the next few years which would stabilize her retirement and allow her to provide financial assistance to her children that they so richly deserved. Her father was ailing. He owned a large home and being an only child; she expected to receive a significant inheritance. However, her father who had been widowed for over a decade had recently married a woman who was twenty years younger than her father. She did not respect her dad's new wife. It was not the fact that she was only a few years older than Conny, but she feared the interest in her father might be financially motivated. It was probable that her father was going to outlive Conny and since his home was jointly owned with his new wife, it is very doubtful the value of her dad's estate would ever be transferred to his granddaughters.

Conny had to address a lifetime of issues in a very short period of time while dealing with her own grief. She never considered an estate plan and believed it was not a priority since most of her family died in their late eighties. In addition to her own demise, Conny believed that she let down John and her daughters. Suddenly her priorities became clear. She had a beautiful backyard and a family she loves. She could spend her final days meeting with accountants and lawyers, but financial issues will take care of themselves, just like always. One question seemed to take priority - is the upcoming pain worth the extra time with her loved ones? She has come to grips with her own mortality, but booking a one-way trip to Belgium could be the best or worst decision she ever made.

Conny was advised on Tuesday by her oncologist that her future was bleak. She knew that she had a short period of time to get her affairs in order since the decisions she made would impact her loved ones. She could not bring herself to start making her final arrangements, even though she knew it was the right thing to do. Whether she was afraid to face her fears or just indifferent, it was not a path she wanted to travel. Her most important priority was to spend time with her family and build her inner strength for the rough road ahead. Conny died in her sleep that evening. It took four months to settle her estate, but since she was not divorced and her ex-husband was the beneficiary of her will, he inherited her home and remaining assets.

Once we retire, it is common to have thoughts of our own mortality. It moves from the theoretical to cold hard reality when a doctor advises we have a terminal illness and our lifespan will be measured in months rather than years. Our first response is normally to fight the disease because we are not ready to leave our friends and family. Often, we start a regiment of operations or painful treatments that may extend our life a few months. We understand that if our physician advises that a disease has a low survival rate, it is natural to pursue any chance to continue living. A doctor's instinct is to prolong lives and to complicate the issue; the medical community is compensated by the number of tests and procedures performed, which may or may not, slow the speed of the patient's demise. It is important to ask a simple question – will the proposed treatment cure my condition, mitigate the pain or extend my life? If the life extension is short and the pain is severe, choose wisely. In many cases, the patient is unable to communicate for various mental or physical reasons and it is left to a loved one to make decisions on the patient's behalf.

Bottom Line - Too many families lack a current will, a power of attorney for financial affairs, a living will, life and disability insurance, an estate plan and have no idea how to fund their retirement. It is common for many families to ignore these financial products as they believe they are not a priority for their immediate future. Retirement approaches and many families have no plan to finance this period of their life that may extend over thirty years. Many people have a plan in their head but seldom memorialize it in writing. If we do not invest a few hours and a small amount of money in preparing for our future, our families may pay a steep price.

CHAPTER TW0

A PORTRAIT OF HELL

Everyone wants to live a long life,
but no one wants to grow old.

Dante Alighieri wrote an epic poem called *Divine Comedy* and the first part was known as Inferno, which is the Italian word for Hell. The book was illustrated by Sandro Botticelli and he became famous for his map of hell. Dante's vision of hell had nine levels or circles. Each had punishments based on certain sins. For example, the second level was for people who were overcome by lust and the final level is a frozen lake containing those who were guilty of treachery. Concepts such as hell are subjective and change over time. There is truth in the adage that one man's heaven is another man's hell.

Before outlining the various types of retirement hell, it is important to stress that longevity is not a form of hell; rather it is just part of the aging process and cycle of life. If we are lucky, or cursed, to have a long life, we shall become frail; our mental facilities will decline and eventually, our life force will leave us.

There is no agreement as to what constitutes an ideal retirement. A wealthy man who loses his wife the day he retires may grieve for the rest of his life. A couple with limited resources and no extra cash for the small pleasures in life may find retirement to be the greatest period of their lives as they are able to spend time with friends, family and each other. Families have different goals and expectations. A number of professional athletes who had a few years of a very high salary, cannot adjust to a lifestyle where the income may be modest, but twice the national average. The inability to sustain the good life has led to bankruptcies and failed marriages.

Once we leave middle age, we must face the fact that our bathroom mirror does not lie. Wrinkles start to appear; our hair starts to gray and maintaining an ideal weight becomes quite challenging. Some people throw large amounts of money at various professionals to keep their youthful appearance, while others accept aging as a part of life that beats the alternative. Many appreciate the beauty of aging, while others seem not to care. As we enter our so-called golden years, we notice the transformations on the outside of our bodies, but it is less obvious the type of changes that are starting to take place on our insides. It happens at various ages and level of severity, but eventually, we all start to decline physically and mentally, unless we suffer an early and unexpected death. This process impacts the quality of our life and even if we are not impacted for a number of years, we may have to care for a partner whose decline has been more rapid than expected.

Levels of Retirement Hell

Retirement hell occurs when we are touched by certain horrific circumstances in our final years. There are five levels of retirement hell:

- Insufficient money to pay for the necessaries of life
- Sad and lonely existence
- Subjected to elder abuse
- Living in a substandard retirement home
- Painful end of life experience

Insufficient Money - A retired individual whose only source of income is government pensions may struggle to pay the necessaries of life. Depending upon whether seniors own their own home or pay rent, there may be insufficient money to pay for accommodation, food and utilities. Cutbacks may have to be made which could include eating less healthy food, rationing prescription medicine or reducing utility usage. This scenario is often worse for those that live alone, especially females. Although circumstances will vary by individual, if government pensions are their only source of income, it is common for many seniors to have an annual income of less than $20,000. Since some government pensions are based on earnings during their working years, those earning low wages or did not work outside the home will receive smaller pensions. Many women from the baby boomer's generation will be hit hard. To make matters worse, they tend to outlive men, so they will have longer periods of low income.

Sad and Lonely Existence - There is a level of sadness or even depression that impacts many seniors. During retirement, especially during the final years, the elderly may deal with issues such as loneliness after losing a spouse or partner, the onset of physical ailments and insufficient funds that restrict their ability to enjoy life. Chronic loneliness is epidemic. The fear of moving to a nursing home and declining mental clarity can make this period extremely stressful, especially for those who must face it alone. When one partner starts to decline either mentally or physically, it may fall upon the other spouse to provide support. It is often challenging to support a high-needs spouse when it is becoming problematic to take care of ourselves. Many seniors face a level of social isolation. Their partner may be deceased or infirm; the children may have moved away or are busy with their lives. Many of their friends and family have either passed away or are suffering from some type of affliction that restricts their ability or desire to interact with others. Social media may provide some escape from the isolation, but this is a generation that prefers phone calls and face-to-face contact as the preferred method of communication. The loss of independence is often the cumulative effect of losing friends, declining mobility and insufficient money. This loss is gradual but quite often limits their ability to enjoy life. Many seniors are proud, independent people and relying on others for assistance goes against their nature. They have spent their lives caring for others and are proud of their ability to handle the circumstances that life has thrown at them. The loss of independence is not an easy hurdle for many to clear, but the issue can be minimized if the person has a strong support structure.

There was a man who was a financially successful executive. He had few friends and he defined himself by his work. Upon retirement, this wealthy executive transformed into a lonely and bitter man with no friends, hobbies or outside interests. He had his own kind of retirement hell that had nothing to do with money.

Aging can cause a reduction in libido, which can be very challenging for some seniors to accept. When genitalia becomes ornamental, rather than functional, it can impact an individual's self-esteem. Many men discover that playing billiards with a rope can be devastating to their ego. Even if a little blue pill is able to restore a little bit of the glory days, the lack of a partner may raise the question - why bother?

Elder Abuse - It takes many forms and is often hidden from sight as the person who should be in a position to report or stop the abuse may be the actual abuser. It includes physical, psychological or sexual abuse and can take place in the senior's home or retirement community. It can also include financial abuse from strangers or family. People with dementia, are prime candidates as they are unable or unwilling to communicate the problem to friends or family. The situation is worse for those who are isolated and do not have family members involved in their life.

Retirement Home Nightmare - In previous generations, when gramma could no longer care for herself she moved in with family. When she needed care, there was always someone to provide assistance. Those arrangements are becoming less common and seniors are now moving to retirement communities or nursing homes. The level of accommodation is often dependent upon the individual's financial resources. There are retirement homes that could pass for resorts with waiters in formal attire taking orders for the daily meals. At the other end of the spectrum, many of us have visited an aging relative in a nursing home where residents share a room with three strangers. All of their worldly possessions have been reduced to a bed, dresser and a curtain to pull in front of the bed. In some cases, there was a noticeable odor when entering the facility and residents are lined up by the front door, often making unrecognizable sounds. The staff is often overworked and may have trouble meeting the hygiene needs of the residents. The meals are modest and one gets the sense that these individuals have been warehoused as they await death. Although there has been a significant improvement in conditions in many jurisdictions, once low-income baby boomers hit nursing homes in record numbers, conditions may not be ideal.

In the past, families with financial resources could place the elderly in retirement facilities with an excellent standard of care. We have entered a phase where there are often waiting lists for suitable accommodation. Imagine twenty-five years into the future when the baby boomers want retirement beds and none are available except for the wealthy or well-connected. As a society, we have under-invested in the necessary long-term care facilities for the elderly. We shall lack long-term beds, support workers and medical services. A shortage of facilities will drive up prices and many seniors may be unable to find appropriate living space, even if they had saved to fund this period of their life.

There is a legal term known as an arbitration clause that is included in many contracts. It is common in technology purchases such as cell phones and computers and the clause can be invoked by hitting the "agree" button or signing a contract. By agreeing to the arbitration clause, individuals give up their right to sue for negligence and any disputes are settled through an arbitration process. On the surface, this may seem reasonable, but it is not necessarily an inexpensive process. Lawyers may be hired and there may be fees involved. The rules of evidence used in court proceedings do not apply and there may be no appeal, except to another arbitrator. So, what does this have to do with nursing homes and retirement? These clauses are becoming more frequent in nursing home agreements resulting in patients giving up the right to sue for negligence.

Consider the case of Sister Irene Morissette who was an eighty-seven-year-old nun who had dementia and was living in a nursing home. She told a worker at the facility she had been raped the previous night. The investigation revealed semen stains and vaginal bruising. She kept her door locked at night; there was no indication of forced entry into her room. Sister Irene was unable to identify her attacker and her dementia made the investigation more difficult. The police were unable to identify the culprit and the nun's family sued the retirement residence for negligence.

The elderly patient had signed a contract that included an arbitration clause, so she gave up her right to seek relief through the court system. There was an arbitration hearing and the defense argued positions that would be inadmissible in a court of law. The arbitrator ruled in favor of the nursing home and there was no further avenue of appeal. It is estimated over a million nursing home patients have given up the right to sue for negligence by agreeing to an arbitration clause.

Painful End of Life Experience - When people think about their final seconds on this earth, it is a common desire to die at home, surrounded by loved ones and in minimal pain. The reality is that many die in a hospital and in the months before death, they may receive operations or other painful treatments that may extend their life by a few months. It may have deferred the inevitable for a short period but subjected the patient to incredible pain before they had their last breath. We should have a plan that includes a living will, power of attorney for financial affairs and discussions with family members who understand our final wishes. Medical procedures can cure a disease, mitigate the pain or extend our life by a period of time. Is it the right decision to undergo an operation when you are ninety years of age and your life may be extended by perhaps another ninety days? If a person does not want these painful life extension procedures, they should tell their family, while they still can.

Bottom Line - For most people, a happy retirement is defined by our health, level of positive social engagement and sufficient financial resources to fund our desired lifestyle. The issue is how much control an individual has over these factors. Our health can be a combination of controllable factors, such as diet, exercise and random factors, such as our genetic makeup and bad luck. People can make reasonable lifestyle choices but may be hit by Parkinson's Disease, cancer, or any number of horrific conditions. In the early part of retirement, social interactions are normally within our control, but as we age and our mobility is restricted, we may need help from friends, family, or community support services. There is a correlation between levels of income and health care services and it has been a challenge to ensure those at the lower end of the economic spectrum receive the medical assistance they require in a timely and affordable fashion.

Growing old is not for sissies and unlimited cash will not change the eventual outcome. However, those who are forced to live their final years in poverty will enter a level of hell that no one deserves. Financial resources do not ensure a happy retirement but living in poverty during this period is a horrible way to spend your final years. Seniors that played by the rules their entire life should never spend their final years making choices between food and medication.

CHAPTER THREE

ROADBLOCKS TO A SECURE RETIREMENT

*Money is a measure of the decisions
that we have made.*

Those at the top and bottom of the income scale have a reasonably predictable path to retirement. Wealthy and upper-income families who have secure employment, beautiful homes, investment portfolios and possibly one or more spouses who are members of a defined benefit pension plan, seldom face financial issues in retirement. At the other end of the economic scale, many individuals have low-wage jobs or survive on government benefits. They must self-finance retirement, yet they are the least able to implement this strategy.

In between the wealthy and the financially challenged is a middle class that is vulnerable to the realities of today's economy. If these families can continue being employed and are saving for retirement, either as members of a pension plan or utilizing the various tax-assisted vehicles designed to promote retirement savings, they may have a financially stable future. However, many working families live from one payday to the next and retirement planning is not a priority. Despite working their entire lives, many retire with no pension and minimal savings. They face the unpleasant task of adjusting their lifestyle in retirement to the amount of government pensions that will be received.

Off-Ramps

There are a number "off-ramps" for families that believe they have a viable plan to fund their retirement. Those with a company pension or a high income will face fewer obstacles, but the middle class may face a minefield of issues as they approach retirement. Potential disruptive forces that could impact a family's plans include:

- Job loss
- Employer goes bankrupt
- Divorce
- Inability to live within your means
- Catastrophic disease, injury or death
- Indifference to financial and retirement issues

Job Loss - When baby boomers entered the workforce, jobs were plentiful and the lack of a post-secondary education was not an impediment to a middle-class lifestyle. During the 1980s and 90s, there were a number of changes in the job market that created havoc for many families. The manufacturing sector was hit hard by free trade, globalization and powerful foreign competition. Plants closed, jobs moved overseas and there were too many workers chasing too few jobs. There was growth in the technology, health care and education sectors. Although many of these newly created jobs were well-paying, they required specific skills and a post-secondary education. Technology has inflicted a two-pronged attack on the middle class. The first shoe dropped around 1990 when the manufacturing sector was hit. The second wave is just starting to occur as technology, robotics and artificial intelligence will eliminate many jobs. The upheaval in the job market will continue and it is unclear which jobs will be safe from innovation and technology. There will be winners and losers in our turbulent future and a family can never be certain how they will fare. Companies will go bankrupt and others will reduce staff because of competition. Losing a job and landing employment with similar salary and benefits may be rare unless the family is prepared to move to other parts of the country.

Employer Bankruptcy – In a world of disruptive technologies and economic turbulence, even large employers face the possibility of bankruptcy. This causes two potential problems for employees. In addition to the loss of a job, insolvency will impact the company pension. Often the pension plan is underfunded and the employer is unable or unwilling to contribute additional cash to the plan. Current employees understand they may not receive the money they were promised, but what about retired employees? These individuals expected a stream of income for life. However, if a company cannot meet its pension obligations, someone is going to get hurt. If a retiree's pension is reduced or eliminated, they probably have spent too many years out of the workforce to find a new job with reasonable pay. It is possible to obtain information on the employer's pension, such as whether or not the pension is fully funded and if not, how much is the shortage? This may be interesting information, except there is nothing an individual can do with this troubling knowledge, except worry.

Many people who self-fund retirement will purchase an annuity with their investment and they are designed to pay a stream of monthly income until the individual dies. What happens if the insurance company paying the annuity goes bankrupt?

Defined benefit pensions are ideal if individuals stay with one employer for most of their career. However, defined contribution plans may be the superior option for individuals who change jobs multiple times or are employed by a company which goes bankrupt. If increased insolvencies are the way of the future, the pension income of retired employees may be in jeopardy.

Divorce – Divorce is painful at any time, but if it occurs close to retirement the financial impact can be devastating.

Homes are sold, assets divided, pensions may be split and support obligations can be generated. If the separation occurs within ten years of the targeted retirement date, there may be insufficient working years to replace the assets that were lost. Both parties to a divorce often suffer a reduction in lifestyle.

Inability to Live within your Means - The world consists of savers and spenders and should two spenders marry, it may be a challenge to stay out of debt or put money aside to fund their retirement. Those who live by the principle of spending less than they make and putting money aside for a rainy day will lay the foundation for a secure future. Lifestyle should be based on family income, rather than satisfying one's wish list by the excessive use of debt.

Some families that were financially secure may have suffered a job loss but do not cut back on their spending. They may liquidate their retirement savings or use debt to maintain their lifestyle. A reduction of income in retirement is possible for the wealthy and the upper-middle-class, but the occurrence is somewhat rare. Even when the wealthy hit these bumps in the road, their retirement may not meet their expectations, but it is still better than most. Perhaps they will not be able to spend six months of the year in a warmer climate or afford to hobnob with former friends and colleagues, but their life will be quite fine by most people's standards.

There are a number of young men working in high-paying jobs such as professional sports, the oil fields or overseas, who have reverse earnings. Unlike most people whose wages increase as they age, these groups may suffer a decline in income over time. Although their income may appear to put them into the category of the upper-middle class, all too often these high-paying jobs do not last long enough to build a financial cushion for the periods of lower income that may lay ahead.

Catastrophic Bad Luck - Bad things happen to good people. The death or disability of a partner can be financially devastating. Although these risks can be managed by life and disability insurance, many members of the middle class either have no insurance or are underinsured. Fortunately, these events are rare, but they can destroy a family's future earning power.

Indifference – There are three types of indifference related to financial affairs. The first group has either no interest or aptitude in financial matters and outsources the activity to a responsible third party. For example, a surgeon may earn a very large salary but has no interest in investing. As long as the bills are paid and the family's lifestyle is maintained, the doctor is not prepared to spend any time on financial planning. He has no expertise and no desire to become educated on the topic, so he pays someone to manage his financial affairs.

The second category consists of individuals that are truly indifferent. It is a form of willful blindness. They are apathetic and only concerned with maintaining their current lifestyle and expect the future to take care of itself. The final group is indifferent to money management as they are convinced there is no payoff for time invested and this is informed indifference. If a family is struggling to pay the bills and there is no money left over for savings or investing, why bother to understand the stock market? Many families at the bottom of the economic ladder believe it is more important to know the rules related to unemployment insurance, disability insurance and welfare, than mutual funds, tax and retirement planning. Perhaps they realize their future will be funded by government programs, rather than self-sufficiency, so their priorities may make sense. Is it possible that some of the disinterest in financial matters is the result of the lack of training and education that we received during our years of schooling?

Bottom Line - For wealthy and upper-income families, retirement should be a time to enjoy the pleasures of life. However, many families that must self-finance retirement lack the financial resources to make it happen. This will be especially challenging for families that defer planning for this stage of their life until the decade before they retire.

For families that survive on government benefits, retirement will be funded by a different source of government income as pensions replace unemployment insurance, welfare or disability payments. Often their income does not change significantly and their lifestyle continues.

.

CHAPTER FOUR

WOMEN AND RETIREMENT HELL

*Dating advice for seniors - the odds are good,
but the goods are odd.*

Women from the baby boomer's generation will suffer a disproportionate level of poverty in retirement. The primary reasons are the gender pension gap and a longer lifespan on average than men.

Gender Pension Gap - The wage gap is still an issue in our country and one of the consequences is a pension gap which results in women receiving smaller pensions than men. The wage gap varies by jurisdiction and industry, but women tend to make on average 85% of a man's salary. However, in cases where the genders have the same job and work for the same employer, men may still have a slight wage advantage. Although there are some cases of outright discrimination, both legislation and the obvious nature of the problem have resulted in reduced inequality. One of the reasons for the wage differential is women have a greater participation rate in lower paying jobs that have fewer promotional opportunities. Many women suffer from a concept known as the "motherhood penalty." Rearing children has resulted in some women making difficult decisions concerning careers and family responsibilities. The high cost of daycare also complicates the situation.

Many single mothers have found that social assistance provides a higher take-home pay than a low-wage job after considering the cost of childcare, while other women have restricted employment opportunities because of affordable daycare. Trying to balance a career and raise a family have resulted in some women choosing to work fewer hours or moving to less demanding jobs. These decisions are often made without regard to the impact on their retirement income.

The gender pension gap is the difference between the amount of pension income received by men as compared to women and it receives less attention than the gender pay gap. Fewer years in the workforce and less income throughout their careers compared to their male peers results in less pension income in retirement.

Longer Life Span - Women from the boomer's generation tend to have a longer life expectancy than males. This has a negative impact on women in retirement. They not only have more years to finance, but the insurance industry pays smaller annuities to women as compared to men. Assume a man and woman are both sixty years of age and had $500,000 in their retirement account when they ceased working. If the decision is made to convert the $500,000 into an annuity, the male will receive a larger monthly income. According to the insurance industry, this is not a form of discrimination since women tend to live longer than men and therefore are paid a smaller monthly amount. Should a woman receiving an annuity die in her first decade of retirement, as opposed to living the number of years anticipated by mortality tables, she receives a raw deal.

If a retired couple's primary source of revenue is the husband's pension, his death may result in a drastic drop in family income. The pension may stop on his death, or the spouse may receive a significantly reduced survivor benefit. In many cases, the surviving spouse will be unable to maintain her lifestyle with the reduction in income. The net result could be living the last decade of her life in poverty.

These issues will mitigate as future generations retire. The pension gap will be significantly reduced as the increasing number of university-educated females in the workforce will be better prepared to fund their retirement. Many families from the boomer's generation were dependent on the husband as the primary source of retirement income, but that model is changing.

Changing Makeup of Families

Although it may be an uncomfortable topic, there is an argument that the mating formula from previous generations was based on inequality. Back in the day, the man wanted sex and the female wanted financial security and a deal was struck. Thankfully, those days have almost come to an end.

When the parents of baby boomers got married, most stayed true to their vow "until death do us part." Even though many relationships were less than ideal, couples stayed together since getting a divorce was often difficult. Those days are long gone. No fault divorce is easy to obtain. Women who become pregnant have options that were often not available in previous decades. It is now socially acceptable for couples to live together without the "benefit" of marriage.

Many older individuals who have experienced the world of marriage, have decided never again. Perhaps the glamor of a big and expensive wedding is a younger woman's dream, or the concept of a new economic partnership is a situation to be avoided for financial or estate planning reasons. If a large monetary or emotional price has been paid to leave a marriage, it may be a legal arrangement that some prefer to avoid. Marriage and relationships have changed over the past few generations, but how does that impact retirement?

Beyond the emotional toll, the closer a divorce is to the projected retirement date, the less time there is to recover from the financial hit of the settlement. Those that get divorced past the age of fifty may have to sell the family home and a downsized retirement may be the result. Couples that are young and in love seldom take the cost of an eventual divorce into the decision-making process as to whether they should marry or live in a common-law relationship. However, divorced individuals in their fifties may find that another marriage is not in the cards, because of the potential cost should the relationship not work out as intended.

Divorce can be a costly process. Assets are split and the former couple must maintain two households. Although some women with wealthy spouses may land on their feet in retirement, many women are negatively impacted. When assets are split, many women share their retirement assets, so they can maintain the family home. There are a number of emotional reasons for making this decision but giving up investments can cause severe financial issues in retirement. When a couple is married and the wife leaves the workforce for a number of years to raise the children, there is an assumption that any eventual reduction in her income from this period would be offset by the spouse's retirement income. However, this is often not the case should the couple go their separate ways.

Consider the case of the Diva Book Club which consists of three divorced women that meet for coffee on the second Tuesday of every month and a discuss a book they have recently read. In reality; it is just an excuse for good friends to get together. They shared a similar lifestyle as the children had left the nest and they were all able to retain their home after their marriage ended. They attend the theatre as a group and enjoy their visits to various restaurants. Their jobs finance their lifestyle and there is enough left over to spoil the grandchildren. As they commenced updating the group on the comings and goings of their life, one woman stated she had visited a financial planner and it appeared that she could never afford to retire. She has no pension and a modest level of savings. Her financial planner advised that her retirement income will be less than $25,000 and the primary source of income will be a government pension. To make matters worse, she is the more financially stable than the other members of the book club. They had all left the workforce to raise children and their financial priority in the divorce was retaining their home. The financial planner advised that selling the home could be a source of retirement revenue. She could reduce spending and maximize her savings, but that would drastically reduce her lifestyle. The Diva Book Club has come face to face with the gender pension gap.

Many divorced women in the later stages of their career may find transitioning from worker to retiree is financially challenging. Although they can maintain their lifestyle while they are working, many women suffer a significant drop in retirement income due to the pension gap. One potential solution to a lack of retirement income is working more years than was originally planned. For example, the goal may have been to retire at sixty, but a divorce can result in working for an additional number of years.

Developing a plan in the decade before retirement often results in nasty surprises and too few years to resolve the issues. This, unfortunately, has become the norm for many women who live by themselves and never took retirement planning seriously. Unless women are wealthy after the divorce settlement, a delayed retirement is the new normal.

Relationships After Fifty

An unmarried woman over the age of fifty may have a different view of men and relationships than she did in her early twenties. Many educated and successful women do not require a man for financial security and may fill their social engagements with like-minded friends. Going out for dinner or to a movie was usually a boy/girl dating relationship in their youth, but now they attend such functions with a group of females. Some women may still desire the classic relationship, but finding the right man can be a challenge. The reason is simple; they are no longer prepared to put up with any crap from men. What they wanted in a man when they were twenty-one is no longer as important. Issues such as the ability to provide financial security or a strong gene pool have been replaced by the desire to find a friend of strong character.

At the other end of the economic scale, some women covet the financial resources a male can bring to the relationship. Unfortunately, many women still have to compromise their principles to achieve a level of security. There is also a role reversal scenario, where many women are providing financial support to men who are unable or unwilling to work.

Change in Relationship Contracts

Most people understand the pros and cons of signing a marriage contract. They are more common in second marriages as couples bring a lifetime of experience to the relationship. In recent years, many older couples have decided to live together and are signing co-habitation agreements. This is an attempt to provide some certainty in case the relationship ends. Since different rules apply to couples that live common-law vs. being married, one party may be financially decimated if they separate during retirement. An individual could walk away from the relationship with no financial support or division of assets. For example, a woman may retire early and move in with her man. If the relationship does not work out, she may be thrown to the curb with little legal remedy available.

Some couples sign such agreements in case the rules of common-law relationships change as governments attempt to make them equivalent to marriages. Such a change in the law could impact the matrimonial home, division of assets and support obligations.

It is not uncommon for parents to suggest their children obtain a prenuptial agreement to protect the child's assets in case of a divorce. Some parents are concerned that future inheritances could be split between their child and an ex-spouse and that notion is unacceptable. Roles are being reversed as children are recommending that their parents consider a prenuptial agreement. The kids are concerned that if an elderly parent remarries, it may reduce their future inheritance. As a result, they strongly suggest that a prenuptial agreement to their parent as it best suits the interests of the child.

Educational Gap

In addition to the gender and pensions gaps, we are now experiencing an education gap that will work in favor of females, except the effect on retirement may be decades into the future. The more immediate impact will be on income inequality resulting from the changing gender makeup of universities. Back when baby boomers were finding mates, many young women saw marriage to a stable income earner as a path to financial security. However, this pathway is in decline. To understand the change, consider university enrolment in the 1960s compared to the present time. Decades ago, post-secondary schools were dominated by males but that trend has reversed and young women often make up the majority of graduates. When universities were male-dominated, they tended to marry women who never attended university since there were few female graduates available. In today's world, with a more even gender split, it is very common for a person with a university degree to marry another person with a post-secondary education.

This union of couples with a higher education has a potential impact on income equality. They tend to have a significantly higher family income than those where neither spouse attended a post-secondary institution. Not only do they have an anchor in an upper-middle-class lifestyle, but their children will have a tremendous advantage over those from lower-income families. They are products of an excellent gene pool that may provide an academic advantage throughout their life. They also have parents that value education so their family income may be effective in knocking down barriers in their children's pursuit of academic excellence. Living in better neighborhoods, attending fine schools, access to tutorial services and participation in activities such as sports and music paves the way for academic success. The most reliable predictors of a child's success in life are the education and income of the parents.

Since university graduates tend to marry each other, the marrying pool has changed over the past few decades. In the 1970s, male graduates tended to marry women without a degree since there were very few female graduates available. However, men with university degrees are currently marrying women with a similar educational background, resulting in fewer women with a high school degree able to pair up with a post-secondary school grad. As a result, one path to financial security for women without a higher education has been significantly diminished. One interesting point is that the number of women who marry men with less education is at an all-time high and this trend is expected to accelerate in the future.

One of the added benefits of the majority of graduates being female is their impact on the workforce as they attain senior positions. In addition to a greater ability to self-fund retirement, as they attain a critical mass, there will be a tipping point that may put a chokehold on harassment and misogyny in the workplace. As a result, women will be less likely to leave a good job because of an inappropriate boss or co-worker.

Bottom Line - If a woman does not have the resources to be financially independent in retirement and will be dependent on her husband's income, it would be wise to consider her options in case of divorce or the early death of her spouse. A combination of the gender pension and wage gaps have resulted in reduced retirement income for women from the baby boomer's generation.

PART TWO

STRATEGIES TO AVOID RETIREMENT HELL

CHAPTER FIVE

SOURCES OF RETIREMENT INCOME

*Retirement is a phenomenal grown-up playland
for those that made good decisions between
the age of eighteen and twenty-five.*

The theory of self-financing retirement is straightforward, but given the potential obstacles facing many middle-class families, the implementation may be challenging. Self-financing requires saving sufficient money to make up the shortfall between the targeted income and the amount that is available from private and public pensions. Governments recognize the importance of this task and have established investment vehicles that allow families to save for retirement in a tax-effective manner. The government's theory is that if individuals maximize their annual contribution to these plans, the resultant income when combined with government pensions, will be sufficient to fund retirement. The theory is straightforward, but there are many obstacles to implementing this strategy, including:

- In order to maximize the benefit of the various tax-assisted investment vehicles, it is important to start contributing at an early age. However, many young men and women who are establishing their careers do not see retirement planning as a priority. It is more common to focus on this objective as they reach middle age. This is often too late to take the maximum advantage of these plans.

- After paying the bills, many families have little money left for savings. Excess funds may be used to pay down debt, save for a new car or a vacation. In many cases, saving for a retirement that is many years in the future is not a priority.

- Even if a family understands the importance of saving for retirement, life has a way of introducing new priorities, such as assisting children with a home purchase, funding a period of unemployment by one of the spouses, or moving to a larger home.

- Any money that has been invested to fund retirement must be prudently managed. Many unsophisticated investors lack the expertise to manage their savings and do not employ professional advisors to provide assistance. Many conservative investors shun equity which makes it almost impossible to earn the necessary rate of return.

Sources of Retirement Income

There are six primary sources of income that families utilize to fund retirement and they are:

- Government pensions
- Private pensions
- Savings and investments
- Equity in the family home
- Receipt of an inheritance
- Income earning activities

Government Pensions - The amount of government pensions are often dependent on one's earnings over a lifetime and therefore workers with higher incomes receive larger pensions. For the sake of simplicity, let's assume government pensions provide an income of $18,000 per annum. Most families would have trouble maintaining their lifestyle if these pensions were their only source of income. Some financial planners suggest that families should target an income of 60% of their pre-retirement income. The struggle for many families will be to fund the difference between the 60% figure and the amount supplied by government pensions.

It is possible to access a government website and determine the approximate payout upon retirement. This is time well invested as it provides two important pieces of information:

- A forecast of pension income.
- Individuals have the option of receiving their pension at various ages. The website provides the information to determine the amounts that will be received based on the dates the payments commence.

Private Pensions - Individuals who are either smart or lucky to be hired by an employer who provides a pension have laid the groundwork for a financially secure retirement. These companies tend to compensate their employees at a higher level than smaller companies, which facilitates individuals increasing their personal wealth by building their savings and investments. Many baby boomers are retiring with defined benefit pensions, while future generations may have either no pension or one of the plans that may generate a reduced level of income. The three main types of pensions are:

- Defined benefit
- Defined contribution
- Target benefit plans

Defined benefit pensions are the gold standard in retirement plans. In the early 70s, they were the most common type of pension, whereas today it is rare to find a company offering these plans to new employees. The exception, of course, is governments, but they play by different rules. These plans were designed in an era when individuals may work for one company their entire career. The employee was promised a level of benefits in retirement based on some combination of salary and years of service. It was the responsibility of the pension to accumulate sufficient funds by means of contributions and investment income to pay the promised level of benefits.

From the employee's perspective, it is the ideal type of retirement arrangement as it includes a predetermined level of payments and a target retirement date. The employer hires professional money managers, so employees are not involved in the investment process. If the assets decreased in value, the employer is responsible for any shortfall. In other words, the individual does not bear the risk if the pension assets decline in value. However, investment risk is a major issue to employers and many firms are no longer prepared to offer these plans. If the stock market crashed, the value of the pension assets would be reduced by a significant amount. If the pension is underfunded, it is the employer's responsibility to contribute cash to reduce or eliminate the shortfall. Many companies are not prepared to spend millions of dollars (or more) to offset a reduction in pension plan assets caused by a decline in the stock market that is beyond their control. As a result, new employees are often required to join a defined contribution plan, where employees make the investment decisions and bear the risk of poor performance.

Defined contribution pensions make no promise as to the amount of pension income retired employees will receive. There is a formula that determines the level of contributions, but the size of the ultimate payout will be dependent upon investment performance. For example, employees may be required to contribute 4% of their gross pay and the employer may match these contributions. Employees will normally make the investment decisions and at retirement, there will be a sum of money which is used to purchase a stream of income, such as an annuity. Investment decisions made by the individual will determine the amount of money available to fund retirement. If the investments underperform because of declining stock values or an over-allocation to fixed income products, the individual will receive a reduced pension.

Target benefit plans are a more recent phenomenon and are a mixture of the two types of pension plans. These plans promise a targeted level of benefits, like defined benefit plans and operate on the assumption the pension investments will achieve a certain rate of return. If the actual investment performance falls below the targeted return, the retiree will receive a reduced pension. Employer's like these plans since they eliminate the investment risk of defined benefit plans and employees receive professional money management.

It should be noted that there is actually a superior type of pension plan than the three types that have been discussed and they are pensions designed by politicians for politicians. They are often combined with a generous separation allowance. These plans are not available to other citizens and they reflect the incredible sacrifices politicians make in order to serve the public.

Savings and Investments - If there is a gap between the level of income needed for retirement and the amount provided by private and government pensions, the difference may be funded by savings and investments. If there is a shortfall, the options are a reduction in lifestyle, selling assets, such as the family home, acquiring debt or deferring the start of retirement. An ideal form of retirement savings are the various registered accounts such as the 401(k) and IRA plans in the United States or Registered Retirement Savings Plans in Canada. Maximizing the annual contributions to these tax-assisted plans is one of the best investments an individual can make.

Home Equity Options - A family that owns a home when they retire have a number of options available to turn the equity in the property into a source of retirement funding and they include:

- Selling the family home
- Home equity loans
- Reverse mortgage

Once the children have left home, the parents may have more space than they require. As they age, they may start to encounter mobility issues and find the upkeep of the home to be a challenge. They can sell their property and move to either a smaller home or rental accommodations and use the surplus funds to fund their lifestyle. One of the surprises facing many seniors is the lack of suitable alternatives. One-floor condominiums may be appealing, but they are not inexpensive. Relocating to a smaller community may make the most financial sense, but if it means moving away from friends and family, the idea becomes less appealing.

A family may decide to stay in their property and transfer the equity in the home into debt. The most common techniques are home equity loans, remortgaging and reverse mortgages. One option is to take out a home equity loan or a line of credit based on the value of the home, but the issue is how and when the amount will be repaid. The family has the option of remortgaging the home to access the equity. The issue with these options is the individual's income level. Once a family has retired and wanted to tap into their home equity, they may have insufficient income to qualify for a loan.

Reverse mortgages are based on the equity in the home, rather than the family's income. To understand the workings of this product, let's assume the home is worth $400,000 and based on the age of the owners and location of the property, the family will qualify for a $250,000 reverse mortgage. Once the transaction has been completed, the family will have $250,000 in the bank and a mortgage of an equal amount on their home. The beauty of this product is the loan does not have to be repaid until the home is sold, the spouses move, or they are both deceased.

A loan that never has to be repaid may sound like an ideal solution, but there is a downside and it is a major issue. Returning to our previous example, if we assume the value of the reverse mortgage was $350,000 and the home was worth $500,000 when the last spouse dies, the beneficiary receiving the home has a number of options. The house can be sold and the proceeds of the sale can be used to extinguish the debt and the beneficiaries retain the balance. It is also possible for the beneficiaries to retain the home by refinancing the $350,000 loan. The family has utilized the equity in the home to fund retirement, rather than leaving it for their beneficiaries. Returning to our example, if the family had one child who will inherit the entire estate and there was no reverse mortgage, the child would have received an asset worth $500,000. However, once the reverse mortgage is eliminated, the equity in the home is reduced to $150,000. A reverse mortgage may be an ideal product for a couple with no children as funding retirement can take precedence over the needs of beneficiaries. Parents must decide if they want to use the equity in their home to fund their retirement or leave it to their children as part of the estate. It's a tough call for many families.

There are concerns with reverse mortgages, such as fees and the rate of interest charged on the loan, but it may be an ideal option for some families. In the United States, there have been some unscrupulous players in this market, so it would be wise to have a lawyer review any contract before it is signed. It is important to have both spouses named on the deed. One area of concern is the date the last spouse leaves the home and thereby triggers the repayment clause. There have been issues when the last surviving spouse moves to a nursing home and therefore the debt must be repaid, even though the owners assumed the debt would be repaid after their death. If there is someone else living in the home when the last spouse dies, that individual may have to vacate the property.

Home ownership can be a source of funding in retirement, but unfortunately, many families will enter retirement and still have a mortgage on their home. This has two significant implications. Mortgage payments can be a major expense in retirement and results in less equity in the home that could have been used as a source of capital.

Intergenerational Support - The baby boomer's generation has accumulated an incredible amount of wealth, most of which will be passed down to beneficiaries. The inheritance may create a cash infusion that will alleviate many of the next generation's financial issues.

The traditional approach is upon the death of the first spouse; the assets are transferred to the surviving partner. Upon the death of the last spouse, the assets would be equally distributed to the children. This approach intuitively makes sense, but let's assume the last surviving spouse passes away at age ninety. When the assets are distributed to the beneficiaries, they may all be in their sixties and retired.

Many parents that have sufficient resources to fund their remaining years may consider gifting assets to their children prior to their death. This strategy has the following potential advantages:

- It provides assets to family members when their need is the greatest. Rather than receiving the inheritance after they retire, the money could be transferred to their children and assist with paying off the mortgage, helping their grandchildren through university or fund contributions to various registered retirement accounts.

- Depending upon the jurisdiction, a prepayment may reduce any inheritance taxes or probate fees that would be eventually be levied on the estate.

- It will result in lower taxes for the parents, as investments gifted to the children will result in a reduction of the parent's income for tax purposes.

- The parents may achieve a sense of satisfaction as they watch their children utilize the funds.

Many parents are challenging the assumption that each child should receive an equal share of the estate. Their reasoning is typically based on one of the following scenarios:

- The children may have unequal needs based on their station in life. For example, one daughter may have married a surgeon and has no financial concerns while the other daughter made some bad choices as a teenager and is a struggling single mom. Do they allocate the inheritance based on need? If they chose this option are they punishing success?

- One of the children is considered the black sheep of the family and leads a lifestyle that is unacceptable to the parents. The child may be into drugs, crime or has chosen to be estranged from the family.

- One of the children may have expended a considerable amount of time and money as the primary caregiver to the parents in their final years.

The child may receive an increased inheritance as a reward for the care that was provided.

- An individual may have entered a second marriage that has resulted in a blended family that includes stepchildren. It is not uncommon for a parent to have a greater concern for the offsprings of their first marriage as compared to the stepchildren of the new family.

There is no perfect solution to the issue of whether or not some children should receive a greater share of the estate than others, but the key is for spouses to discuss the issue and ensure their estate plan addresses the concerns of both parents.

Although some parents are in the fortunate position to infuse a significant amount of cash into their children's lives, others are not as fortunate. Many families have minimal savings, but if they own a home, it can be a future inheritance to their children. This becomes problematic if the parents need to utilize the equity in the home to fund their retirement. In such cases, there may be few assets for eventual distribution to the children.

Income Earning Activities - Retirement is not necessarily a time when individuals cease all forms of income earning activities. For example, some may decide to work part-time or if they own a small business; they could continue in a reduced role. Rental income can be a great source of income in retirement and the eventual sale of the property can provide a source of cash to fund their remaining years. Some seniors with a larger home than their needs dictate, have found that renting a room is a valuable source of income. However, many landlords must deal with tenants from hell and may wish they never made the decision to become involved with rental income.

Although some may work in retirement to attain a level of personal satisfaction, others return to the workforce because they need the money. Regardless of the motivation for working, the concept of retirement as a fixed date when all work ceases is an outdated concept. The number of seniors employed in the workforce is at an all-time high and the financial constraints of many families will ensure this trend will continue for the foreseeable future.

Bottom Line - Unless a family has a high level of income or has at least one spouse that is a member of a pension plan, it will be challenging for a family to set aside sufficient funds to meet their targeted income in retirement. A significant segment of our population will rely on government pensions as their primary source of income. This is not only an issue for the families, but it will create a financial burden for the government who will be required to provide health care and ensure lower-income families have a lifestyle that is consistent with the values of our country.

One of the greatest mistakes a family can make is to not calculate their potential income in retirement. If it is discovered they have inadequate income to maintain their lifestyle; this issue must be addressed long before the anticipated retirement date. In such cases, the family home may become a necessary source of revenue, but that may result in major lifestyle decisions.

CHAPTER SIX

CAN YOU AFFORD TO RETIRE?

No good deed goes unpunished.

There are three streams of individuals that will transition into retirement. The first consists of wealthy and high-income families that seldom encounter financial issues. At the bottom of the economic spectrum are individuals that have lived on various forms of government assistance throughout a significant portion of their adult life. Their retirement income will consist of government pensions replacing other forms of social assistance. The majority of families fall somewhere between these two groups. If a family member worked for a company that offered a pension, the combination of employer and government pensions might provide a reasonable level of income. Families that are neither high income nor members of a pension must self-finance their retirement or exist on government pensions.

Those without pensions are often the least able to save for retirement. They may retire with a mortgage remaining on their home and outstanding credit card debt. The reality is that many families struggle to live on their current earnings and will face a reduction of their modest lifestyle once they quit working.

Let's Do the Math

If a family has any concerns that they will not have sufficient income, they should prepare a forecast of their retirement revenue. The ideal approach is to visit a financial planner or accountant who can who perform a detailed calculation. There are a number of excellent professionals that charge by the hour vs. those that offer a free retirement forecast if individuals purchase their mutual funds. The advantage of using these services is they can calculate various "what if" scenarios. For example, they can quantify the impact of taking government pensions at a later date, provide an overview of your tax situation and assume various rates of return on investments.

An alternative to using a financial planner is to develop an income forecast by combining pension income and with the application of the 4% guide to investments. It allows individuals to ballpark their retirement income and get a sense if they can afford to retire. An advantage of using this process is that it forces individuals to research certain information such as the amount of government and private pensions that may be received. This information is available on company or government websites. Although this formula is free and quick, the best solution is still the use of financial planning software.

Before reviewing the math, it is important to understand three concepts:

- The 4% Guide

- Rule of 25

- Rule of 15

The 4% Guide - It was an idea developed by Bill Bengen who graduated from the Massachusetts Institute of Technology. It is a rough guideline that allows families to determine the rate which investments should be liquidated, so they last at least thirty years. It assumes a balanced portfolio and concludes that the ideal strategy is to withdraw 4% of the family's nest egg every year during retirement. In each subsequent year, the 4% would be increased by the rate of inflation to maintain purchasing power. For example, if a family had a $1,000,000 in savings, they should withdraw $40,000 per year.

It is not a perfect guideline and there have been changes since it was devised. We have had an extended period of low-interest rates, plus life expectancies are increasing. It assumes linear withdrawals, but a family's cash flow needs can vary from year to year. Corrections to the stock market and their timing can impact the size of the nest egg. Do not accept the 4% rule as gospel. However, it can provide insight.

Rule of 25 - This calculation allows a family to determine the amount of capital required to achieve their retirement goals. Multiply the annual investment income required times twenty-five and this is the size of the target portfolio. If the objective is to generate $100,000 of investment income per year, they should target a portfolio of $2,500,000 and utilize the 4% rule, i.e., $2,500,000 @ 4% = $100,000. This raises an obvious follow-up question as to how they are going to save the amount of capital required.

Rule of 15 - Multiply your final salary times 15 and that will indicate the amount of investments required to generate investment income equal to 60% of your pre-retirement income. Assume an individual's final salary was $100,000.

$100,000	X	15	=	$1,500,000
$1,500,000	X	4%	=	$ 60,000

A Ballpark Calculation

Step #1

Desired Retirement Income $_____   (1)

Step #2

Sources of Income

Government Pensions $_____   (2)

Company Pension $_____   (3)

Savings (using 4% guide) $_____   (4)

Anticipated Retirement Income $_____   (5)

Step #3

Difference between steps #1 and #2

      Gap or Surplus $_____   (6)

Notes

1) This amount is the desired level of retirement income. A common goal is 60% to 70% of pre-retirement income.

2) Total government pensions anticipated. The amount can be adjusted based on the age individuals apply for the benefit.

3) This is the amount of private pension income. Employers can provide an estimate of the amounts that will be paid.

4) Multiply the estimated savings at retirement times 4% and this will suggest an amount to be liquidated on an annual basis.

5) This is the total estimated retirement income from the government, private pensions and savings.

6) This is the difference between the targeted level of income that is desired at retirement less the forecasted sources of revenue. A gap requires an action plan to eliminate the income shortfall.

Caveat - The 4% liquidation of savings will include a drawdown of capital, plus the investment income earned in the year. Income tax complicates this calculation as the various sources of income are taxable, except for withdrawals from savings accounts and cashing guaranteed investment certificates. It is more informative if the numbers are translated into after-tax figures using an individual's tax rate, but this complicates the calculation.

The Formula - A Case Study

Fred and Marilyn were in their late 50s and were hoping to retire in five years. Although neither had a pension, they had always lived within their means and had savings of $200,000. Their mortgage had been eliminated and they had no credit card debt. From a financial perspective, they thought they would be in a position to retire, but they never pushed the numbers. Fred currently makes $60,000 per year, while Marilyn earns $40,000. They believe they could enjoy their retirement if they had a combined income of $60,000 and were confident they were in a better financial position than their friends and neighbors. They both worked full-time and lived by the doctrine of spend less than you make and save a portion of each pay for a rainy day. They did the math and were surprised by the result.

Step #1

Desired Retirement Income	$60,000

Step #2

Sources of Income

Government Pensions	$35,000
Company Pension (if applicable)	$ n/a
Savings (using 4% guide)	$ 8,000
Total	$43,000

Step #3

Difference between steps #1 and #2

Gap	$17,000

Since they are $17,000 short of their annual goal, they need to increase their savings over the next few years. They used the "rule of 25" to determine how much they need to save:

Shortfall times 25

$17,000 X 25 = $425,000

The 4% rule is applied to the balance:

$425,000 X 4% = $17,000

To meet their objective of an annual income of $60,000 and retire in five years, they need to save $85,000 per annum for the next five years, i.e., $85,000 X 5 = $425,000. This was not going to happen when their combined gross income was $100,000, so they must develop plan B.

Fred and Marilyn raised a family, paid for their children's education and skimped on the luxuries of life so they could retire in their early sixties and enjoy a well-deserved retirement. They were proud of saving $200,000 and living debt free. Financially, they did everything right and now realize they cannot meet their goals. It appears they either live on less than $60,000 per annum or work a few more years so they can increase their savings. One of the advantages of projecting a family's retirement income is that it can initiate a discussion between the spouses as to their retirement plans. If both spouses are committed to funding retirement, a solution may be feasible. However, if one partner has no interest in increasing the amount of the family's savings by cutting back on lifestyle expenditures, the problem may not get solved, but at least they know where they stand.

The couple in this example had a combined income of $100,000, a mortgage-free home and $200,000 in savings. In the world of families without pensions, they would appear to be significantly better off than most and yet they still came up short on the necessary income for retirement.

Retirement and Working Families

Once we are within ten years of retirement, we have a sense of how our future will unfold. Many working families who are not members of a pension plan and have minimal savings face a challenging future and saving for retirement will be a difficult, if not an impossible task. Less than 50% of families that are within a decade of retirement have at least one spouse who is a member of a pension plan. As a result, many families will survive on government pensions as their primary source of income. However, many of these families may have access to three potential sources of retirement funding - equity in the family home, future inheritances and ongoing income-earning activities.

In retirement, many working families will face similar circumstances as individuals that lacked full-time employment throughout their adult life since both groups will rely on government pensions as their primary source of income. This latter group includes those with a disability, plus individuals who lack the skill, opportunity or interest in maintaining full-time employment. These individuals will have government pensions to replace their current sources of income, such as welfare, unemployment or disability payments. The average amount of a government pension approximates $18,000 per year, give or take a few thousand dollars and varies based on an individual's circumstances.

A demographic spike known as the baby boomers will soon be entering retirement homes. We have too few beds and our health care system will be stretched to the limits to care for this group prior to their demise. If a pensioner is surviving on $18,000 per annum ($1,500 per month) and has to move to a nursing home or assisted living facility, are there any residences in the country that charge less than $1,500 per month? Either the government pays the shortfall, or the individual will face a crisis.

56

Bottom Line - This chapter outlines a ballpark approach to forecasting retirement income. The ideal approach is to use a financial planner or retirement software to make the necessary calculations. It is foolish to enter retirement and then discover the available income does not meet your needs. Invest the time to forecast your retirement income and if there are issues, it is best to be aware of the future that awaits you, unless the issues are addressed while the family is still in the workforce. It is common for individuals to have a target retirement date. It may be based on reaching a certain age or number of years of service. These dates are often selected in conjunction with the company's pension plan. A more sensible approach is to select a date when the family has accumulated sufficient financial resources and eliminated their debt.

If I gaze into my crystal ball and attempt to forecast the of age retirement in twenty years, it will be an ugly situation. It would not be surprising, if the average age of retirement for the haves is under sixty, while the average age for the have-nots is over seventy. Income inequality will become entrenched as many workers will struggle to survive if government pensions are their only source of income.

Retirement, what could go wrong?

CHAPTER SEVEN

REDEFINING RETIREMENT

Even a broken clock tells the correct time twice a day.

Once upon a time, retirement meant the cessation of work and most workers retired in their mid-sixties. Those days are gone. The date of retirement often depends on an individual's financial situation and some never retire until their health limits their options. Depending upon a family's circumstances, retirement can be heaven or hell. Retirement has gone through a number of changes in the past 125 years. Before World War One, men worked until they were physically unable to carry out their duties of employment. After the Great Depression, governments started to construct a social safety net and unions led the charge to obtain pensions for workers. After the Second World War, sixty-five was the standard age of retirement. As boomers started to retire, the wealthy and those with excellent pensions often left their jobs in their mid to late fifties. A retirement age of sixty-five was commonplace when boomers entered the job market, but it has become somewhat rare as they exit the workforce. Unfortunately, many individuals were forced into early retirement by circumstances beyond their control as companies downsized and they lacked suitable employment options.

The traditional concept of retirement is either dead or dying. Many people do not want to retire. This includes individuals who cannot afford to quit working, plus those that enjoy their job and are not financially compelled to work. Entrepreneurs and farmers are two groups that may work as long as their health permits. Even those that retire from their primary job may still seek some type of post-retirement employment. Although some may work to supplement their income, others enjoy the social aspect of a job or volunteer their time to support a cause in which they believe. Some employees would like to slide into retirement, rather than having a firm date. This is known as phased-in retirement and employees may work only a few days a week in their final year, rather than a full work week. This could consist of job sharing or special project work.

Changes in the job market impacted the age of retirement. Those with financial security could often choose their retirement date, but many that were negatively impacted by the economy continued working by necessity. Companies were able to reduce costs by changing their employment model. Rather than hiring employees and offering the possibility of life-long employment with a pension and benefits, there was an increased use of part-time and contract employees. Many companies wanted employees that fit their core competency model and outsourced non-essential jobs. A reduction in pension benefits resulted in more families financing a greater share of the cost of retirement. The lack of a pension tends to increase longevity in the workforce as families require more years to accumulate the necessary savings to finance their retirement.

Redefining the Term "Old" - Over a hundred years ago, many men stopped working as life had worn them down. That world has changed and many retirees are traveling the world, have an active sex life and are socially engaged. We hear expressions such as "age seventy is the new fifty." This does not apply to everyone, but the days of retiring and waiting to die are long gone.

A retirement date may be chosen by an individual, or it can be forced upon workers by circumstances beyond their control. Another factor that can impact our potential retirement date is our health. There are men and women in their seventies who run marathons, while a number of people in their thirties smoke and suffer from obesity. They ignore physical fitness and struggle to walk a hundred yards at a brisk pace. As marathoners attempt to break the two-hour barrier, Fauja Singh completed the Toronto Waterfront Marathon in eight hours and eleven minutes. Mr. Singh was a hundred years old at the time. Some people are able to work at a high level in their seventies, while people in their thirties and forties appear to be on a fast track to a lifestyle supported by disability income long before their normal retirement date.

Given that individuals have different levels of physical fitness and financial resources, the concept of a predetermined retirement age is an outdated concept. Many jurisdictions have eliminated mandatory retirement. Governments have responded to this new reality by allowing individuals to select the date they want to start receiving their monthly retirement pension. There is a "normal start date," but the monthly payments are increased if the start date is deferred or reduced if the individual wants to receive the pension at an earlier date.

Retirement should start when certain goals have been accomplished, rather than the arrival of an arbitrary date. Ideally, it should commence when the family has sufficient savings and they no longer desire to participate in the workforce on a full-time basis. However, part-time work may carry on for years. Assuming individuals want to retire, the date should be decided by their circumstances, although this may be inconsistent with the needs of the employer.

Early retirement may have been popularized by the baby boomers, but the world has changed and that privilege may soon belong to the wealthy, upper-income families and members of strong government unions. Many employers act on the assumption that individuals want to retire, but that may not be true. If a family has to self-fund retirement, saving the necessary capital can be very challenging and retirement may be deferred due to economic necessity.

Bottom Line - Based on the changes in our economy and the revised definition of what constitutes "old," retirement is no longer a line in the sand that separates working and non-working years. We are moving toward two separate spheres of retirement. For those that have a high income or an excellent pension, early retirement is a possibility. For those that lack wealth or a pension, expect a return to the retirement model of 1900. Economic necessity will result in individuals working as long as they are physically able or until no employer wants their services. Most of these jobs will be low paying with few benefits, but it is the price to be paid to put food on the table.

CHAPTER EIGHT

JOB STRATEGIES

*The harder a person works, the more
difficult it is to surrender.*

The key to self-funding retirement is staying employed. Baby boomers often worked the majority of their career for one company, while those who recently entered the workforce will deal with a different world than the one enjoyed by their parents. Cradle to grave employment has become less common and a lack of job security has become the new normal for too many workers. There is a risk that new technologies could make almost any job disappear.

People feel helpless if their jobs are eliminated by circumstances beyond their control. It is easy to understand their frustration, but the changing job market raises the importance of everyone taking responsibility for their career. Back in the good old days, like the 1980s, most large employers would invest in employee training to assist in upgrading their skills. The current focus appears to be ensuring employees are compliant with government laws and regulations, plus there is a greater emphasis on the soft skills, such as leadership and working in a diverse culture. If individuals have to pay the cost of their training and educational updates, they may not be inclined to invest the necessary time and money. Many people have a different view of training if the cost comes out of their pocket. As my grandmother used to say - it makes no sense to be penny wise and pound foolish.

Developing a Job Strategy

The first step in developing a personal job strategy is to determine the degree of risk that your job may be eliminated, through no fault of your own. Consider the job market to have four segments:

- Highly skilled
- Medium-skilled - protection
- Medium skill - no protection
- Low skill

Highly skilled workers are the least vulnerable. If their job disappears, they decide they hate their boss or want to move to another part of the country; their skills will land them on their feet. Included in this group are lawyers, doctors, engineers, nurses, experts in technology and professional accountants. This is the ideal segment, as the pay is high and job opportunities are usually available. Funding retirement is seldom a problem for this group.

Medium-skilled workers can be quite competent, but their skills are often specific to their employer and may not be transferable to another job. If the employer is doing well financially, employees may have a long career, but they can be vulnerable to changes in technology in either their job or industry. Workers that have some form of protection are less vulnerable to the realities of the economy or a boss from hell. The most common form of protection is membership in a union, but it can also include seniority, being the boss's son, or having a relationship with an important client. Medium-skilled jobs with a lack of protection are vulnerable to job loss. When such a loss does occur, it can be a challenge to find an equivalent salary and benefits in the same community in a timely fashion.

Low-skill workers tend to work for minimum wage or a few dollars more per hour. Training is often completed during the first day of work. These jobs may have high turnover, low pay, few benefits, part-time hours, short notice on scheduling and few possibilities of promotion. They are often in industries such as fast food, retail, agriculture and landscaping. Although they may be ideal for students or those seeking a few hours of part-time work, the pay is barely adequate to raise a family and totally insufficient to self-fund retirement.

The skill possessed has an incredible impact on the level of pay and job security. It would seem obvious the path to a better job depends upon a person's skill, but too many people are unable, or unwilling to upgrade their skill set. One reason for this view is the belief that education and skills are acquired before entering the workforce. That may have been true fifty years ago, but those days are long gone. Education and the acquisition of job-related skills must be a life-long process. Unfortunately, upgrading takes time, money and can be tremendously inconvenient. Too often, workers take the position that if the employer is not prepared to pay for the necessary training, then why should they use their time and money? The issue is who is responsible for your career - you or your employer? Unfortunately, people who cannot figure out the correct answer to that question may struggle to find a well-paying job that lasts until retirement.

Long-term success in the workforce requires skills, a work ethic and a moral compass. If acquiring a skill means going back to school, borrowing to pay the tuition or an intrusion on your personal time, then that is the price to be paid. Even if an individual has minimal money, most programs offer financial assistance. Perhaps a person feels they are too old to go to school, or their peers are not supportive, but unfortunately, most people can find an excuse that validates their inaction and helps their journey on the path to nowhere.

Value of a Skill - The fewer people that can perform a skill, the greater the value in terms of compensation. There are a handful of quarterbacks in the NFL that make about twenty million dollars per season. There are approximately a hundred quarterbacks in the league and a few hundred playing in the NCAA. Why does this small group make such a phenomenal salary? There are the only people on the planet that can perform at such an extraordinary skill level.

It is not your outstanding personality or the promise to try your best if only given the opportunity that leads to better jobs; it is the possession of skills valued by employers. Whether it is acquiring a trade, computer programing, or repairing motors, the acquisition of hard skills are vital to a career. Knowledge of your employer's methods and procedures and your perceived innate ability to lead people may hold little value in the job market.

There is a secondary advantage of possessing a skill. If a job does not work out as planned, either because it has been eliminated or does meet your expectations, your skill may be valued by other employers, or it may provide entrepreneurial opportunities. If a plumber with a high school diploma and a human resources manager with an MBA who works for the federal government both lose their job on the same day, expect the plumber to find work quicker than the MBA.

Entrepreneurial Option

When I was hired by Price Waterhouse, I was assigned to small business files to assist with their accounting, income tax and financing issues. Fresh out of university, I did not have the slightest idea that I was totally green behind the ears. Other than the professionals, such as doctors and lawyers, I was constantly amazed at how many rich and successful entrepreneurs were of average intelligence. These small business owners came from all walks of life and shared a number of common traits. They took a risk to become an entrepreneur, they understood their customers and worked an incredible number of hours to launch their business. However, there was no consistency in their background or education, except that a university degree was not common. Starting a business means risking your capital and wearing multiple hats from marketing to accounting. Many started their business while they had full-time employment elsewhere. The motivations were diverse as some wanted to kiss their current boss goodbye, others wanted the opportunity to earn a high income, while others followed a dream.

If the objective of starting a business is to generate cash flow as the family's employment situation is less than ideal, it is important to understand what is at risk if the venture fails. In such situations, you can afford to waste your time, not your family's financial security. If your home is promised as collateral for the business, it may be lost in a very short period of time. Institutions that provide financing are experts at protecting their investments. It is too easy to throw caution to the wind as your enthusiasm for an opportunity appears within your grasp. Individuals that have limited capital and cannot afford significant losses should consider establishing businesses that they can walk away from with only a minimal financial loss. Loans, long-term leases and asset purchases are problematic for businesses that do not succeed.

Observations on Starting a Business - Entrepreneurship is an alternative to employment. Despite the potential financial upside and ego satisfaction, the risks are real and if the new venture is unsuccessful, it is possible to be in a worse financial position than if a business had not started. The following are some observations on starting a small business, rather than working for the man:

- Succesful small business owners tend to have expertise in a product or possess business acumen. Consider the example of Steve and Terry who both wanted to start a business as they were worried about the stability of their current job. Steve was a locksmith working for a small family business, but it was only a part-time job. He became an expert in all aspects of locksmithing and started taking some private jobs in the evenings and weekends and eventually started his own small business. Terry was an accountant who wasted his days implementing global accounting systems. The work was boring and no one understood how he could find satisfaction in this job. Terry wanted a change, so he also started a locksmith business. Not only was Terry not a locksmith, but he struggled with anything mechanical and did not know the difference between a deadbolt and a mortise cylinder. Terry took another route to entrepreneurship. He hired two locksmiths and focused on marketing his brand. He later sold his Terry Locks as a franchise across the country. Steve and Terry took different paths to entrepreneurship, but both are thriving in their new endeavor.

- Individuals that are successful in their careers may start a business for a spouse or child who is underemployed. This may be an ideal match for an individual with business acumen and a family member with time.

- When considering the franchise option, remember big money is made selling, rather than purchasing franchises. There are zillions of companies touting themselves as the next McDonalds, but for every golden arches story, there are thousands of "Fluffy Pizza and Sushi Bar" franchises available. Never purchase a franchise unless the proposed transaction has been reviewed by an accountant or lawyer, to ensure the investor does not overpay for something of minimal value.

- Multilevel marketing is a great way to make a few hundred dollars and see how much your friends really like you.

- Never assume you can borrow money and walk away from a failed business venture without repaying the debt. Financial institutions are quite competent at recovering outstanding loans.

- Be leery of using your home as collateral for a loan. A failed business can result in a loss that hurts the entire family.

- Many successful entrepreneurs fail on their first attempt. However, they were committed to success and learned an important lesson. When you fail, fail fast and move on.

- If your marketing program is based exclusively on social media, expect rave reviews from your friends, but few customers. If friends believe they are marketing gurus because they can post on social media, do not have great expectations of generating profit. After their social media campaign flops, they may attempt appeasement with the hollow argument that at least they created awareness.

- Whether it is classed as a business or an investment, a rental property can be an excellent asset to finance retirement. It will provide rental income and eventually can be sold to generate a major cash infusion. Normally these properties are purchased with debt, but over time the mortgage is reduced and the value of the property increases. There are certain skills required to be successful in this business from picking the

69

appropriate property, ongoing repairs and dealing with tenants. It's not for everyone, but it has been a significant source of wealth creation for many families.

- Individuals that have been both an entrepreneur and an employee understand that a day that you lost can be better than a day that you won. Self-employed people may find a bad day in their own business is more satisfying than successes achieved on behalf of an employer.

Bottom Line - Who is responsible for your career? A job strategy is straightforward. Master a skill, stay current on technology and approach your job with a moral compass, a work ethic and gravitas. This may be obvious to those that have experienced success, but it can be too much of an inconvenience for individuals that are locked into an existence where their future may be in jeopardy and are not prepared to take the necessary steps to ensure they have employable skills. Spend the time and money to invest in your career; the payoff can be incredible. A two thousand dollar investment in skills upgrading may be a better investment than purchasing shares in a company.

One job strategy that has proved successful over the years is to align your career with some type of economic power. This can include union jobs, large multi-national companies or governments. The pay, benefits and job security tend to be higher than the packages offered by small employers.

CHAPTER NINE

INVESTING

Wealth creation can be achieved by focusing on long-term greed.

Marion was a typical senior. Although she had a modest amount of savings that had been squirreled away from years of thrifty living, she was not prepared to take any risks with her money. It was not important that the current bull market was producing returns of over 10% per year. She did not understand the stock market or care to learn. She is very happy receiving a return of less than 2% on her guaranteed investment certificates. Deep down, she was not sure she totally trusted banks and probably would have been comfortable hiding her money under the mattress.

Many retirees and working families have no expertise or interest in investing. For families that are self-financing retirement, it is important to develop an investment strategy. Although some people see themselves as a budding Warren Buffett, they often do themselves a disservice if they do not access the expertise that is available in the marketplace. The stock market surged for the decade after the 2008 financial debacle and almost everyone in the market was able to make money. A rising tide lifts all boats, or in other words, even low functioning know-it-alls were able to prosper.

The four factors that determine the ultimate value of a retirement nest egg are:

- Asset allocation
- Which investments will be included in the portfolio
- Investment advisors
- Fees

It is important to differentiate saving and investing. Savings are used to pay for expenses in the next few years, such as a new vehicle or roof repairs, while the objective of investing is to create wealth. Savings are normally liquid investments such as bank accounts or guaranteed investment certificates, while investments may include stocks, bonds and exchange-traded funds.

Asset Allocation - In simple terms, there are three broad classes of assets - equity, fixed income and cash equivalents. Asset allocation refers to how investments are proportioned to these various categories. If investors were fully invested in equity, they might gain or lose 10% of their portfolio in a given year. If they were fully invested in guaranteed investment certificates, they might earn less than 2% on their investments, but they have only a minimal risk of losing money. The rate of inflation should be taken into consideration. For example, if a GIC pays 1.5% in the current year, but the rate of inflation is 2%, there may have experienced a loss of purchasing power. Risk takers may have 80% of their portfolio in stocks, while the risk-averse may refuse to own equity investments. There is no generally accepted standard allocation formula, but a 60% allocation to equity would be typical. Some investors reduce their equity allocation as they age since they want to incur less risk as they approach retirement.

The asset allocation strategy is the foundation of an investment portfolio and is often involves interaction with an investment professional or a robo advisor if you do not prefer the human touch.

Specific Investments - Once a decision is made as to the appropriate asset allocation strategy, specific investments must be selected. For example, the equity component could include individual stocks, mutual funds, or exchange-traded funds. The focus could be on large North American companies or small-cap companies located in the emerging world. It seems investors have a zillion equity options and there is an army of advisors with finely tuned crystal balls to provide guidance to their clients.

Very few investors purchase individual bonds for inclusion in their portfolio, rather they select from the multitude of bond funds that are available. These funds may be either mutual funds or exchange-traded funds.

Investment Advisors - Many families lack expertise in investing and perhaps have no interest in the topic, so they may avoid equity investments or outsource managing their portfolio to a third party. There are incredibly gifted advisors in the marketplace, while others are sales reps that present the client with a menu of mutual fund options and earn a commission on any sales that may result. The key is to find a trusted advisor and this can be difficult for a novice investor to determine who best suits their needs. A good place to start is the recommendation of financially sophisticated friends who are satisfied with their advisor.

Fees - Most investment professionals are very skilled and deserve to earn a fair level of compensation, but from the investor's perspective, how do they ensure they receive value for fees paid? The investment industry has utilized a unique revenue model and it has worked well for the investment advisors. Most professionals, from lawyers to plumbers use an hourly rate to determine their fee for services. Although the investment industry earns fees from transactional charges, such as buying or selling stocks, the mutual fund side of the industry earns vast amounts of money from the management expense ratio (MER) that is included in mutual funds. For example, if an individual owned $1,000,000 of mutual funds, that had a 1.5% MER, the annual charge would be $15,000. It is irrelevant if the portfolio increases or decreases in value, the advisors receive their 1.5%. This is the "piece of the action" model that was perfected by the mob over eighty years ago.

The first step in determining if an investor is receiving value for the money spent on fees is to quantify the amount on an annual basis. Many successful families are quite content to outsource their portfolio management to professionals and do not focus on fees. In a bull market that is growing by double digits each year, it is easy to be satisfied paying a 1.5% fee, or higher. However, there may be better options that charge significantly lower fees.

Meeting with a Mutual Fund Sales Rep

There are incredibly talented financial advisors and others who are commissioned sales reps selling mutual funds. This latter group has a standard sales pitch for novice investors and although it had worked well for years, the theory that mutual funds will solve all your financial problems is problematic. The classic mutual fund sales pitch works as follows:

Environment - The financial planner's clothes and demeanor have an aura of professionalism and the office walls are covered with charts with arrows pointing skyward.

Credentials - The advisor will state that he works with some of the brightest financial experts in the world and has access to their products.

Opening Caveat - The meeting normally begins with a statement that past performance does not guarantee future returns and then will deliver a sales pitch that consistently ignores this sage advice.

Opening Sales Pitch - The advisor will provide information on various mutual funds that had great performance over the last five years and implies that these funds would continue to grow, ensuring a secure retirement for the investor. The advisor has apparently forgotten the earlier caveat that past returns are no guarantee of future performance.

Risk Analysis - Clients will be asked to answer questions on their tolerance for risk to determine how much of the portfolio should be allocated to equity. It appears that in many cases, the risk analysis does not materially change the advisor's recommendations. The standard results are clients under the age of forty-five should have 70% in equity, those over forty-five, but not yet retired should have 60% of their portfolio in equities and retired individuals should be in the 50% range. As luck would have it, financial planners can select from their menu of mutual funds a number of equity options that fit the client's profile as these funds will provide growth, a diversified portfolio and only a moderate level of risk.

Recommendations - The investment advisor may represent over a hundred equity mutual funds, but only recommend those that had the best performance in the last ten years and imply these will continue to provide the greatest capital appreciation. Apparently, he keeps forgetting the past performance and future returns comments that were emphasized at the start of the meeting. If fifteen of the funds were losers, they could be kept in the drawer until their performance improves.

Responding to Challenges - If the client challenges the advice; advisors tend to strut their expertise and state their world-class research department believes the product will do well in the long run. If questions are asked such as why is the recommendation for a 40% bond allocation when most forecasts expect interest rates to rise in the near future, there is a standard response to all such questions. The typical answer is that their experts in head office are certain that a bond purchase was still reasonable in the circumstances because it will provide a conservative investment and provide a level of safety if the equity market declines.

Final Thought - As clients leave their office, they should recall the famous quote from Fred Schwed who admired all the yachts in New York owned by the bankers and brokers and asked the famous question - where are the customer's yachts?

Avoid Actively Managed Mutual Fund

Mutual funds provide diversification and are managed by incredibly talented professionals. They are the cornerstone of many family's portfolio and have provided a great return in the past few years. Despite these facts, many investors will no longer purchase actively managed mutual funds. For those who want a simple answer to why these investment products should be avoided, the answer is because Warren Buffett says so. He is smarter and more successful than you, me and most professional stock pickers. Mr. Buffet believes indexed funds will outperform actively managed mutual funds and history appears to be on his side.

Mutual funds had their day, but exchange-traded funds are a better option. The fees are significantly lower than actively managed funds and academic studies indicate they continue to outperform mutual funds. This position is debated by those in the mutual fund industry that sell these products, but consider the following:

- Attempt to find someone outside of the mutual fund industry that supports actively managed mutual funds over indexed funds.

- Review the performance of exchange-traded funds compared to actively managed funds and it is clear that exchange-traded funds continue to outperform.

It is important to understand the difference between exchange-traded funds (ETF) and actively managed funds. ETFs track a specific index such as the Dow or the S&P 500. The fund owns the same stocks in the same proportions as the index, so it mimics the result of the index, less a small management fee. An actively managed fund tries to beat the index by using their stock picking expertise. Since the active funds charge significantly higher fees, they must beat the market by the amount of their fees to achieve the same return as the index. In any given year, some active funds will outperform indexed funds, but it is difficult to outperform over a period of years.

Investors should work with a professional to select which exchange-traded funds or indexed mutual funds are appropriate for their circumstances. There is a multitude of indexes that can be benchmarked against, so the investor can take a vanilla approach and mirror the Dow or select more complex indexes such as those that track small-cap stocks. If you hear the argument that the financial planner's actively managed fund will outperform an exchange-traded fund, you may be well advised to find another advisor.

Caveats for Rookie Investors - Novice investors are motivated to achieve a high rate of return, but they must avoid the following potentially costly mistakes:

- A financial planner may suggest that the profit can be maximized by taking out a loan on your home and using the proceeds to purchase additional mutual funds. If you receive such advice, your best option is to run. Run hard, run fast. Leverage is a tool for sophisticated investors, but the losses can be significant if the market turns.

- Although banks have marketed their image as trusted advisors, they are really in the business of selling products which are often available elsewhere at a lower cost. If you are purchasing a mortgage from a company other than a bank, ensure your lawyer reads the agreement before it is signed. There may be a cost saving, but there are some bad actors in the private mortgage business.
- Avoid any investment that guarantees a rate of return that is higher than the cost of borrowing. If the rate is guaranteed and above the borrowing rate, why do the vendors have to deal with strangers to make a sale? They should go to the bank, borrow tons of cash and buy the product themselves as the rate of return is so high and the risk is very low.
- Avoid unsolicited investments. When approached by an unknown investment sales rep, hang up the phone, delete the email or sic the dogs on him if he comes to the door. The bottom line is the seller may be a scam artist and the investor is the sucker.

Bottom Line - There are three important takeaways from this chapter. The most important is that families who self-finance their retirement must have an investment strategy. Secondly, unless the investor has attained a level of expertise on the subject, an investment strategy requires the input of an investment professional, which should not be confused with a commissioned mutual fund sales rep who may operate under various titles, such as a financial planner or investment advisor. Finally, regardless of how conservative a family's views are on investing, if the objective is to build a portfolio to fund retirement, it would normally include equity investments.

CHAPTER TEN

EDUCATIONAL STRATEGIES

True inner peace is achieved when we are part of
something greater than ourselves, be it family or a cause.

Prior to the Second World War, the level of economic inequality resulted in children from wealthy families having an incredible head start in life. Their parents had money and connections which ensured their children attended the finest schools. The majority of families were dirt poor and struggled to eke out a living. Then a miracle happened. As the greatest generation returned from the war, soldiers wanted wives, families, homes and big boy toys. A strong middle class was being created. There was a massive economic expansion and for the first time in history, success was no longer directly related to their parent's situation. In other words, the circumstances of their birth would not determine whether or not they would be successful. The playing field was level and kids from working-class families could flourish if they took advantage of the available opportunities.

Those days have ended. Cradle to grave employment is disappearing, technology is eliminating many jobs and newly created well-paying positions are being filled by a young and talented workforce. Low-skill jobs abound, but the level of pay makes raising a family a challenge and self-funding retirement almost impossible.

The Educational Paradox

A post-secondary education is the traditional path to high-paying jobs. University graduates make more than high school graduates and students with multiple degrees earn more than those with a bachelor's degree. However, an argument can be made that most of the courses we have taken are a total waste of our time. There is no issue that we require a certain level of literacy and mathematical skills, but most of our basic education is completed by the time we graduate high school. For those attending a university or community college, there are two streams of courses - job-related and general knowledge. Courses that teach skills valued by employers, such as law, medicine, carpentry or engine repair, can lead to a financially secure future. However, the study of French poets or the history of the Roman Empire is primarily of value if one wants to teach these courses. Graduating with a degree in the liberal arts may result in a high level of debt, but without the acquisition of any job-related skills. Perhaps it increases the student's human capital, but the truth is that most of the information we were taught is soon forgotten and brings minimal value to our lives.

Why should students incur debt and take courses of no practical value? The answer is straightforward; if they are unable to be admitted to a skill-based program, a post-secondary degree is better than no diploma. In addition to the pay premium for attaining a diploma, some employers will only hire individuals with degrees, even though it may not be required to do the job. The ability to acquire a degree requires a certain level of persistence and indicates to employers the student is at least of average intelligence. Students about to enter a post-secondary institution should decide what skills they want to pursue before they make their program selection. The best career choices from a future income perspective tend to be in the professions, such as medicine or law, or a STEM degree. STEM is an acronym for Science, Technology, Engineering and Math. The better the school, the more valuable the degree. In addition to the knowledge acquired, employers know it is difficult to be admitted into these programs and success is the result of above average intelligence and hard work.

At the other end of the spectrum is the liberal arts degree which all too often is the fast track to a job at Starbucks. Despite efforts by universities to try and sell the value of critical thinking and the importance of writing essays that are formatted in the Chicago Manual of Style, they tend to teach skills not valued by employers. Many of these kids are incredibly gifted, but if their only skill is intelligence, most of the other applicants for the job will also be smart. They require skills to stand out from other candidates. Intelligence is a commodity and not a skill that results in premium job offers. Liberal arts graduates, often do not get their career on track immediately after graduation and may work at a few part-time jobs before they land on their feet.

Employers value soft skills such as commitment, maturity, time management and problem-solving skills. Although liberal arts graduates may believe this is their strength, there are two issues with this belief. These skills are almost impossible to measure in the hiring process and there is no reason to believe that a general education will give students a head start in acquiring these skills as compared to those with a skills-based education.

If students are applying for a job with a large employer, they should understand their first interview is with a computer that rates the applicants. The lack of a degree often means the job seeker will not make the first cut. Preference is often given to those with advanced degrees.

Assisting our Children

Most parents would be very satisfied if their children could achieve both a level of happiness and financial security. Most baby boomers are in a better financial position than their parents, but our children may not be so fortunate. We want our kids to be financially successful, but how do we pass on the wisdom we have accumulated in our journey through life? Effective communication with our children is complex and even if we have sage advice that can be shared, many are unwilling or unable to act upon our counsel. Some children appreciate the advice while others may have no interest because of the source. Some live for the moment, while others excel at kinesthetic or tactile learning and may only find out if the stove is hot by touching it. We want to help them to become financially astute, but how do we achieve that goal? Children are unique creatures, so there is no cookie-cutter formula to assist them in their financial journey through life. Even the best advice in the world may be ignored. Parenting books are filled with tons of articles on how we can teach our children the basics of money management. These articles suggest that children should be paid an allowance, they should not be paid an allowance, they should be forced to save 50% of any money they earn and should make their own decisions concerning money. There is a lot of advice, but it does not appear that academic research supports any particular strategy since what is successful for one child, may be ineffective with another.

Any financial advice that is shared may or may not impact the child's future handling of money, but even if parents are totally ignored by their child, it is still time well wasted. There are two old-school money management rules that were developed during the depression era and are still relevant today. Spend less than you earn while saving a little for a rainy day. The second rule is do not buy something just because you want it, rather defer the purchase until you can afford it. These money management tips were obvious to our grandparents, but the advice has fewer followers in our world of instant gratification and easy access to credit. The key is for parents not to parrot these rules, rather they should live by the values they are trying to teach. Children are more likely to emulate behavior they see as successful.

Regardless of whether parents have any useful information to share or the kids have the desire to listen, there is a tremendous opportunity for our educational system to teach the basics of financial planning. We teach our elementary school children how to calculate the area of a scalene triangle, but not how many years it would take to pay off a credit card if we make the minimum payment. Children should understand that borrowing money at 24% on a credit card is foolish and that a hundred-year mortgage on a home may lower the monthly payments, but the amount of interest to be paid increases significantly.

One of the additional benefits of teaching money management in our school system is that the public will be better able to recognize some of the malarkey that politicians try to sell to ensure they remain in power. This includes deficits, bridges to nowhere and the magic beans belief that budgets will balance themselves. Politicians attempt to further their political agenda by continually spending more money than they raise in taxes. Sadly, this strategy is successful since it appears consistent with the views of the electorate.

New Educational Model

Once upon a time, young men and women completed their education and entered the workforce. Other than professional jobs, the employer would provide the necessary training. Those days are coming to an end. Given the rate of change in the economy, education and training must be a lifelong process. Those with skills have to stay current and those that are underemployed need to upgrade their skill set. If training is completed on employees' personal time and they must pay the cost, many people are not motivated to make the necessary investment. The educational model of the future is lifelong learning, but it is possible only the successful will adapt to this paradigm shift.

Until the educational system changes its focus and emphasizes skills rather than facts and abstract theories that are often forgotten soon after the course ends, many students will have wasted their time and money. The problem is what other choices do they have?

Bottom Line - Despite the value we place on sharing wisdom with our children, the most important gifts a parent can provide are supporting their educational journey and an inheritance. If the parent's financial position allows them to prepay the inheritance, it may increase the probability their children may enjoy a financially secure retirement.

PART THREE

OUR FUTURE

CHAPTER ELEVEN

WAREHOUSING GRAMMA

Science has slowed the dying process,
not the aging process.

One of the great comedians of our time is George Lopez. He was born in Los Angeles and is very proud of his Mexican heritage. Much of his humor is based on observations on how Mexicans and Latinos are viewed in America. He claims that if you visit a nursing home, there are no Latino patients, just staff. Where are the Mexican grandmothers? They are at home with her family and if she falls, her grandson will pick her up. There has been a change in our approach to caring for elderly family members over the past few generations. It was once common to have multiple generations living in the same home. On family farms when the parents became too old to continue running the business, it was often taken over by a family member, usually the oldest son. Mom and dad would continue living on the farm, in part because there was nowhere else to stay. It was not just the lack of nursing homes that resulted in multiple generations living in the same home but caring for elders was a key component of family values in bygone eras.

Back in the day, there was a concept of the family built on the belief that parents would raise the children and help them become established in life. Once they became old and needed assistance in their final years, the children would provide the necessary care and comfort. Times have changed. In previous generations, the elderly often had limited financial resources, but a new generation of successful baby boomers have resulted in options that were not available in the past. The rapid expansion of retirement communities has provided alternative accommodation for the elderly. Governments provide pensions and financial support for seniors who reside in nursing homes. Many families are separated by distance and a busy lifestyle that may restrict their ability or desire to have elderly family members move into their home. It is a common comment to hear friends say that they love their mother, but they could never live with her.

Although financial independence has provided options for many seniors, we will face a retirement housing crisis in upcoming decades. The massive demographic spike known as baby boomers will enter retirement in record numbers. Many are financially independent and living the life of Riley. (If you are familiar with the expression "life of Riley" there is a good chance you are only a few years away from considering retirement living options.) As boomers move out of their homes and into one of the various retirement alternatives, they probably assume there will be somewhere for them to move. Unfortunately, that assumption may not be true.

There are currently waiting lists to enter many retirement facilities and the situation will become much worse unless we start to make more beds available. In addition to beds, older patients will flood our health care system. Will we have the resources to meet the needs of our seniors or do we make hard decisions and ration medical services? Advances in medical science may add a few years to our lives, but we may be unable to stay in our homes as we become frail and unable to look after ourselves. If science is unable to cure or slow down the incidence of dementia or Alzheimer's disease, the problems will be compounded.

The Numbers

Waiting lists are becoming common for retirement beds and vary by region and type of accommodation. For example, there may be separate lists for private rooms, government-subsidized accommodations and facilities to care for Alzheimer's patients. Seniors currently on waiting lists were born in the late 1920s or 1930s. What is remarkable about this period is that it had one the lowest birth rates of the century. By examining birth rates and adjusting for immigration, we can get a sense of how many people will need a retirement home for their final years on this earth. We currently have waiting lists for a period of low birth rates and minimal immigration. Many members of this generation did not live long period past their retirement date. Smoking was common and medical care was light years behind today's standards. We shall be totally overwhelmed when baby boomers need accommodation over the next two decades. The cost of health care for this generation's final years will require extensive government spending. Baby boomers were the luckiest generation in history but paying the expenses of their exit will be a significant burden on the generations that follow.

In the United States, approximately 10,000 individuals reach the age of sixty-five every day. This works out to about 3,650,000 per year. Not all of these individuals will move from their home into some type of retirement facility as some will die earlier than expected while others will be able to stay in their home. In the next two or three decades, we will have a massive number of seniors who require retirement facilities, many of which already have waiting lists. Perhaps the private sector will take advantage of this opportunity and start building more retirement homes, but in most cases, the private sector is looking for paying customers and many seniors will lack the financial resources to move into a private facility. It will be the government's responsibility to care for this large segment of our elderly population.

A basic rule of economics is that when demand exceeds supply, prices can be expected to increase. In many communities, there will be a shortage of beds, so just being able to afford a bed, does not mean one will be available. However, there could be a space available in a community over two hundred miles away. Governments understand the issue, but the main thrust of the problem is a decade away. There is still time to find solutions, but they are expensive and the government has many other priorities. Do we believe they will be up to the task?

Retirement Accommodations

As we review the types of retirement accommodation, consider it through the eyes of both the haves and the have-nots. If a family has sufficient resources, they have options, but if their sole source of income is government pensions, they will lack the funds to pay for the assistance they require. An individual whose only income is from government pensions will have an annual income of approximately $18,000. This may vary by a few thousand dollars based on an individual's circumstances, but $1,500 per month is inadequate for any type of retirement community.

Some seniors move if their home no longer meets their needs, while others sell their home to access the equity to finance their final years. When seniors require assistance with living arrangements or want to move out of the family residence, their options include:

- Home care
- Retirement community
- Assisted-living accommodations
- Non-traditional options
- Nursing home

Home Care - Seniors who want to remain in their residence may eventually require some level of home care.

Assistance may be provided by family members or paid professionals. If a senior requires either daily or twenty-four-hour care, the cost may be beyond the means of a family living on government pensions, unless community support is available. Many people are working while caring for aging relatives and this may create considerable financial and emotional stress. Many employers will accommodate employees who are providing such care, but unfortunately many do not. As a result, some families must choose between their job and the care of an aging parent.

In addition to home care, seniors may require assistance with paying bills, picking up groceries and rides to appointments. Many seniors have friends and family that provide support, but an increasing number are on their own with no help.

Bonnie's mother did not want to move to a nursing home and wanted to stay in her own home, but she required full-time care. Bonnie was able to find a support service that could provide 24/7 for the reasonable price of $30 per hour. At least she thought the price was fair until she pushed the numbers and realized $30 per hour works out to $262,800 per year.

Retirement Community - Some couples believe that selling their home and moving into a retirement community will augment their lifestyle as they will enjoy proximity to other seniors and various community-based activities. Typically, residents have private accommodations and access to services, such as meal preparation, transportation and various activities. These accommodations can be expensive and are beyond the means of many families.

Assisted Living Accommodation - Another option is assisted living, which provides some level of medical assistance in addition to the other services. However, once an individual requires increased medical care or assistance with personal hygiene, the patient's needs may beyond the scope of the facility. In such cases, the individual will often transition to a nursing home.

Non-traditional Options - In a few years, families with sufficient financial resources to move to a retirement community may be unable to locate a suitable living space as too many baby boomers are chasing too few beds. A lack of acceptable living quarters will present seniors with a number of options, but most of them are bad. Do they move to a retirement community that is less than ideal or do they move away from friends and family to find a suitable place to live in another community? Perhaps they could move in with their son if their daughter-in-law promises not to jump off the nearest bridge.

Many families face a cash shortage in retirement and seek a less costly place to call home. This may mean moving to a smaller home or apartment, but more extreme options are available. A number of families have decided to move permanently into an RV and spend their retirement touring the continent. For those that find this life exciting, it may be a phenomenal experience while they are in their sixties, but it may be a short-term solution. As both the RV and the drivers age, it is unlikely they will still be touring when they reach their eighties. Moving south and living in a trailer park is an option. Expect growth in condominium trailer parks geared to seniors that will provide a sense of community. This may appeal to some seniors once they sell their home and can take advantage of inexpensive living arrangements.

Expect an increase in hybrid lodgings. For example, there may be apartment complexes where residents occupy a private room but share a common kitchen. Such arrangements may have medical staff available on a rotating basis and the kitchen staff could prepare meals.

Nursing Homes - This type of accommodation provides medical support and takes care of the patient's total needs and focuses on those who are incapable of caring for themselves. Most will meet the grim reaper after they are transferred to this end of life depository. It will be a challenge for nursing home staff to provide the necessary care if private owners force cutbacks and ration services to maintain profit levels. There are three paths to a nursing home. Seniors may move directly from their residence to a nursing home, there may be a retirement community that served as a residence prior to the nursing home, or the individual may be transferred from a hospital. As we shall discuss later in the chapter, these final two paths to a nursing home can be problematic.

Retirement Accommodation Issues

A family may be able to relocate to an ideal independent living community that suits their needs. However, eventually their health will start to fail and they may be forced to move as they require greater care than the staff at their current residence can provide. Now what? On reasonably short notice, they must find a new retirement bed and the options may be limited. It another decade there may be an absolute lack of space regardless of the finances of the family. Couples that leave the family home in retirement should plan for two moves. The first is to an independent living space, but when their health fails they may have to move to a nursing home.

The transition from living in their own home to the various types of retirement accommodation has potential issues for a family, including:

- The timing of the transition
- Impact on the spouse

The Timing of the Transition - There are many beautiful retirement communities, but they are not inexpensive. Private apartments, recreation facilities, swimming pools and exercise rooms are common. This is an ideal spot for individuals who no longer desire or are able to live in the family home and are financially secure. These retirement accommodations provide various levels of medical support, but guests are responsible for their personal hygiene.

When an individual is unable to dress, bath or use the bathroom independently, he or she may no longer qualify to live at the residence since the individual may require a greater level of medical care than the facility can provide. As a result, elderly residents must move to a new location that can accommodate their deteriorating condition. The next residence may be a nursing home which is significantly less desirable than the former residence. One senior described the transition as moving from the penthouse to the outhouse.

Who decides when the individual must transfer to another facility that can better manage his or her needs? The answer is often contained in the contract that was signed when the senior moved into the retirement lodging. The contract often provides the management of the facility the right to decide when residents must move. This decision may be made in a fair and impartial manner, or it can be arbitrary. Imagine the feeling, when seniors receive a knock on the door and are advised they have to exit their current home in the next thirty days. Whether they have somewhere to move may not be relevant to the conversation. Someone else may decide when your time is up.

Before moving into the retirement home, it is imperative to read the contract that outlines how and when the resident will be asked to leave. Does it require a doctor's determination or can the manager of the facility make the decision independently? When one moves into a retirement home, it is time to start planning the next stage of your life as there may come a time when you are no longer welcome at the facility.

Impact on Spouse - A retired couple will face various medical issues as they age, but they do not impact spouses at the same time. For example, one spouse may require assistance, whereas the spouse is full of life and enjoying every day of retirement. If the husband starts to decline physically and money is not an issue, home care is usually the first option considered. However, if a greater level of assistance is required, the couple will face a number of difficult decisions.

Fred and Sue are in their seventies and retirement has far exceeded their expectations. Their children have successful careers and they enjoy an active social life. They live in a beautiful home and do not have a financial care in the world. Fred's health was deteriorating and it was a struggle for Sue to provide the necessary care. The family doctor recommended that Fred move to a retirement community that could better address his medical issues. It had a comfortable one-bedroom apartment, numerous amenities and an on-sight medical staff that could accommodate his needs. Fred begrudgingly accepted the fact that a part of his life was coming to an end. Although Sue was outwardly supportive, she faced a dreadful decision. Does she leave her home and move into a small apartment or does she stay in the home and visit Fred regularly? There was no good answer as it appeared they were separating when they were very much in love. Since Sue lived her life with a family first philosophy, they sold the family home and moved into the retirement community. Although she said nothing, she was devastated by her new lifestyle, that she believed was forced upon her.

After six months in their new residence, Fred's health turned for the worse and the retirement community could no longer meet his needs. Fred transferred to a nursing home and Sue was stuck in an apartment that was never her home. She moved out of the retirement community and rented a small apartment. In the space of a year, she lost her husband, her home and her social life, which was the price she paid for putting Fred's needs above her own. When a spouse requires additional care to the point his or her lifestyle is disrupted, the impact on the healthy spouse should not be underestimated.

Impact on Hospitals

Many hospitals beds are filled by elderly seniors whose needs would be better met if they were moved to a nursing home. However, if no beds are available in nearby nursing homes, patients may be kept in the hospital taking up space that could be better utilized for other patients. Overcrowding in hospitals can be a byproduct of a lack of available nursing home beds. Maintaining a senior in a hospital as there are no suitable options is very expensive. However, it is often a price that is paid because we lack suitable alternatives.

When families reach a point they can no longer look after a loved one; they are faced with the issue of finding suitable accommodation. The number of boomers in frail condition will soon overwhelm the available senior living accommodations and palliative care facilities. Families face a major crisis if they cannot provide care and there are no spaces available. Many families that are denied accommodation struggle on, but some use a tactic of last resort. They call an ambulance and have the family member sent to the emergency ward of the local hospital. Once the patient is assessed and possibly treated, the family advises they can no longer provide care and the health care system is forced to find accommodation. This often results in a placement in less than ideal conditions, but many families believe they have no other option.

A New Concept - Senior Ghettos

Given the growth in the number of seniors looking for new living facilities, both entrepreneurs and large companies will step into the void. Many seniors survive on government pensions and it will be a challenge to find room and board within their limited budget. The private sector may start to build more retirement lodgings, but many seniors have an annual income of less than $18,000. If the government does not foot the bill, they may be clustered together in less than ideal circumstances. This may lead to the start of senior ghettos. Is it unreasonable to expect that some of these companies will hire less than competent staff and lack the resources to supply nutritious meals for their clients? One strategy to maintain profits would be cut back

on money spent on meals. Can we be certain that no company will cut back on medication or medical services? Will there be sufficient personal care workers to take of a resident's hygiene needs at 3:00 am? Perhaps we would be less concerned about the inevitability of senior ghettos if we had any assurance that we would not be living there in a few years.
.

Future Retirement Communities - We need a massive influx of new retirement beds and the private sector is capable of delivering large scale accommodations with military-like precision. What design features should be built into large-scale retirement communities that can meet the needs of baby boomers who are retiring in massive numbers?

> **Safety of Residents** - If individuals with dementia or Alzheimer's disease are intermingled with seniors who are still mentally competent, some degree of separation and security are necessary. It may sound funny to hear stories of night screamers or grandpa walking around with no pants, but it can be truly terrifying for those who live in such an environment. Locks on the doors, video surveillance and security guards can help assure the safety of seniors living in the retirement homes of the future.

> **Visitors** - Although visitors are key to a client's enjoyment of the facilities, restrictions would have to be in place to ensure only people with a valid reason to be on the premises are allowed access. It is unacceptable to allow homeless people to walk in off the street and help themselves to the supper buffet or steal the residents' possessions.

> **Outside Recreational Area** - A park-like setting would be ideal for seniors to get some daily exercise. Since some may wander off, it is important the area be securely fenced for the safety of the residents.

Meals - A large buffet may be the easiest way to keep costs in line and still allow the guests to socialize during meal time.

Medical Services - Rather than sending patients to the nearest hospital by ambulance, the facility would have a medical ward with nurses on duty at all times.

Does this describe a large-scale retirement residence or a new super prison that can hold our most dangerous offenders? Perhaps the companies that run private prisons in the United States can expand into retirement communities, as it may be consistent with their current business model.

Bottom Line - It appears that warehousing and medicating our seniors will be a part of our future. Those with financial resources may be unable to find accommodation if we have a serious bed shortage. Families surviving on government pensions will require additional assistance to pay for the increased care they require. It will be a financial challenge for the government to provide the resources that aging boomers require. I fear the term senior ghettos may be a part of our future.

CHAPTER TWELVE

THE CHANGING JOB MARKET

Everything that can be invented has been invented.
Charles Duel Commissioner of US patent office - 1899

In my previous book - *Retirement Hell - Byproduct of a Middle Class Under Siege*, an explanation was provided as to why baby boomers were the luckiest generation in history. They were born into a world of opportunities and economic growth. There were three paths that boomers could follow to achieve a level of financial success and lay the foundation for a secure retirement. The higher education path was followed by many successful boomers and the formula was straightforward:

- Obtain a university degree. The field of study was not important as there were jobs for every graduate, whether it was a degree in business or children's literature.
- Work for a top-tier employer that provided a pension, benefits and opportunities for advancement.
- Have a moral compass and strong work ethic.

There was a second path for young men who did not pursue the higher education option. They could have a financially secure future if they acquired a union job, took an apprenticeship, had a career in law enforcement or firefighting. When boomers were entering the workforce, women faced many roadblocks to a high-paying career. University was often not an option, but those following this route had a tremendous head start. Their path to success in the 1960s and 1970s was to become a nurse, teacher or marry well. Although these three paths to success served the boomers well, sometime around 1990, the world started to change. The growth of free trade and advancements in technology significantly reduced the number of medium skilled manufacturing jobs. However, the higher paying jobs that were being created required specific skills backed up by a post-secondary education.

Back in the day, boomers were born into a world of opportunity. In addition to the financial security that was afforded this generation, many believed they had a hero's journey. Rising from working-class families, they had to blaze their own path. Many young men and women came from families with various parental issues, yet they rose above these obstacles and found success. When we compare our journey to that of our children, we believe our path was more challenging. In some cases, this was true, but most times success was achieved if individuals took advantage of the multitude of opportunities that were available to this generation.

Our current job market works against lower-skilled individuals. Although these jobs are plentiful, the pay may be minimum wage or slightly above. Many are part-time and the number and predictability of hours can be an issue. Raising a family and saving for retirement on this level of income is just shy of impossible.

Although technology eliminates many jobs, it does create new opportunities. However, we are facing an issue known as the transition dilemma. As new technologies make certain jobs obsolete, those losing their jobs are often from working families that lack a post-secondary education, while the jobs being created are filled by highly skilled graduates. Manufacturing was hit hard by technological change. The future will see an acceleration of this trend as artificial intelligence and robotics continue to be introduced.

It is difficult to predict which jobs will be disrupted or eliminated by technology. Consider the case of the indoor shopping mall. A few decades ago, it was the hub of many community activities. In addition to shopping, there were restaurants, movie theatres and a place for teenagers to hang out. Amazon's incredibly efficient online shopping model has decimated many malls. When was the last time an indoor mall was built in your community? It is true that Amazon has created a massive number of jobs to manage their shopping empire and this includes warehousing, shipping, customer services, etc. The problem is that the brick and mortar stores which are hurting are in your hometown. Although Amazon may have over 350,000 employees; they are probably located elsewhere. If we have driverless vehicles within the next decade, that will be catastrophic for those working in the taxi industry and truck drivers. Money managers and real estate agents are also in the crosshairs of technological disruption. Robotics and artificial intelligence will run factories with fewer employees. They are also being introduced into surgical procedures, which may impact both the remuneration and staffing requirements in our hospitals. It is a challenge to think of any job that is safe from changes in technology.

If technology continues to eliminate jobs for working families, how do we create meaningful opportunities for those that lost their source of income? In theory, these workers can be retrained, but a thirty-five-year-old high school graduate taking courses in computer technology has very long odds of beating out applicants with degrees in technology, engineering or similar fields from post-secondary institutions. The workers who were laid off because of technology must be retrained so they can earn sufficient income to fund a middle-class lifestyle, rather than taking a six-month course that prepares them for entry-level jobs in competitive industries. When workers are retrained, the government sponsoring the program declares success, while the individuals suffer a major reduction of income. This results in the goal of saving for retirement being put on the back burner.

Government employment that traditionally had a high level of job security also face potential risks. Not all branches of government have been a model of financial responsibility and this presents two very real dangers. If a government decides to get its financial house in order, staff may be reduced as departments are eliminated and branches are merged. Outsourcing is a potential source of downsizing, but government unions have been reasonably successful including language in their contracts to restrict this option. The second risk public service workers face is new political leadership coming to power and promising reduced government, lower taxes, balancing the books, draining the swamp or some other slogan that puts the target sign on the back of government employees.

The best path to a secure retirement is either a high-paying job or one that includes a pension. To benefit from membership in a pension, especially a defined benefit plan, requires staying with the same employer for most of one's career and that is becoming more challenging in our ever-changing job market. A job strategy depends upon your age and position in your career trajectory. People who have been in the workforce for twenty-five years tend to have a career path that has been laid out by their circumstances. At this point in their career, it can be a challenge to change employers and receive an equivalent compensation package. Too many people that thought the grass was greener on the other side of the fence find out to their dismay that the job did not turn out as expected. Some leave because they are unhappy with their boss and do not heed the wisdom that sometimes the devil you know is better than one you do not know. For many middle-aged workers, the key to a secure retirement is maintaining their current job.

Jobs from the Employer's Perspective - Prior to the 1980s, most jobs were full-time, while part-time work was primarily filled by our youth and women looking for a few hours work outside the home. Many part-time jobs were in the restaurant industry, where staffing requirements need to be varied throughout the day. Back in the day, summer jobs were common as students earned extra income to support their education. Those days are over. Employers started to realize they had hiring alternatives and the most expensive option were full-time employees. Non-permanent staff offered the following potential advantages:

- They are often paid less than full-time employees.
- A part-time employee may receive no benefits or a lesser amount than full-time staff. This could be a significant saving if the employer provides pension benefits.
- If a part-time employee had to be terminated, it was normally significantly less costly.
- If the employer was able to classify workers as self-employed, they would be able to avoid the various payroll taxes, such as social security, unemployment insurance premiums and workers' compensation.
- If the workload was not consistent through the year, part-time workers offered increased flexibility. Companies can hire employees with the skills they require, rather than investing in training and education.
- Contract work is also a test period for future full-time employment as it allows the employer to evaluate an individual without making a commitment. If the employee is initially hired on a contract or part-time basis and does not meet the employer's expectations, the perceived hiring mistake can be resolved at little cost.

These are legitimate advantages that accrue to the employer, but to the detriment of employees. What started as a trickle in the 1980's has turned into a gusher of part-time and contract work, especially for young adults who are attempting to get established in their career.

Once companies mastered the advantages of part-time employees, they commenced concentrating on their "core competencies." This term refers to focusing on activities that are strengths and eliminating or outsourcing functions that are deemed less important. For example, many companies decided that payroll was not a function consistent with their core competencies, so they eliminated the department and hired a payroll services company. Departments that were either eliminated or outsourced included corporate security, printing, customer support and tech support.

Bottom Line - In addition to technology and artificial intelligence causing havoc in the job market, the nature of work is changing to the detriment of workers. The concept of cradle to grave employment is becoming less common. Young adults often have to work a few years at part-time or contract jobs until they are able to get their career established. Older workers are being pushed out of their job earlier than they had planned. Full-time employment is a key success factor in raising a family and funding retirement. Those days appear to be over for many workers. Working part-time or having frequent periods of unemployed may result in savings being used to fund family living expenses rather than a source of income in retirement.

.

CHAPTER THIRTEEN

THEN AND NOW

How many of our greatest successes
were the result of unanswered prayers?

The cornerstone of a secure retirement is a full-time job lasting until individuals retire at a time of their choosing. Ideally, they are members of a pension plan or earn a sufficiently high salary to self-fund retirement. This plan was much easier for baby boomers than the generations that followed. The following factors work against younger workers achieving a similar level of financial security in retirement as the boomers enjoyed:

- The continued decline of pension plans
- Reduced time in the workforce
- Ongoing government financial stress
- Contraction of business locations
- Introduction of a gig economy

The Decline of Pension Plans - Companies are starting to question whether or not they want to be in the pension business. There was a time when employees worked their entire career for one employer and there was a sense of family in the corporate culture. Employers in the private sector realized they bore a significant investment risk, so many companies have phased out defined benefit plans. Although some offer defined contribution pensions, others have no interest in offering any type of retirement plan to their employees. Public unions have been very successful at protecting their member's pension benefits since politicians want to avoid the prolonged labor strife that eliminating these pensions would cause. The final shoe will fall if companies decide they only want to commit to employees for a few years and therefore retirement funding should be exclusively the employee's responsibility. Individuals can use their pay to purchase an automobile or save for retirement; this is not the employer's issue. Dupont was one of the first large companies to cease making contributions to their employees' pension plan.

Then

The majority of baby boomers who graduated from a post-secondary educational institution or worked at a union job had a pension. This resulted in financial security for many members of that generation.

Now

Except in government jobs, new employees are seldom able to join a defined benefit plan. Fewer companies are offering pensions resulting in more families having to self-fund retirement.

Reduced Time in the Workforce - Once upon a time, individuals graduated from high school or post-secondary school and entered the workforce. Their career often lasted over forty years. However, the number of years of full-time employment in the workforce is being reduced for many individuals and this can significantly impact retirement funding. For those entering the job market, finding full-time employment may not occur until a few years after graduation. University graduates may juggle multiple part-time jobs until they can launch their career. Individuals entering the workforce directly from high school may take jobs that pay slightly above minimum wage. The net result is that it takes longer to get a foothold in the adult world of career and family. Living expenses can consume most of a paycheck and the decision to purchase a home and have children may be deferred for a few years. It is currently commonplace for individuals to start a family in their thirties, while their parents often started in their twenties. This impacts retirement as the kids leave home and the mortgage is paid off closer to the start of retirement and this negatively impacts the level of savings in the family's peak earning years.

The job market will continue to change to the detriment of many employees' retirement. Advancements in technology can result in an employee's skills becoming outdated in a short period of time. Some employers may be inclined to hire younger individuals with the required skills, rather than attempting to retrain older workers. Many individuals become unemployed later in their careers due to some type of economic restructuring and are unable to replace the income of their former job.

Then

Boomers graduated school and started a full-time job. Many worked an uninterrupted career for the same employer.

Now

There may be an extended period between graduation and finding suitable full-time employment. It has become common to work for multiple employers and there may be periods of unemployment. Economic restructuring in its various forms had resulted in workers being forced to retire before they were ready. Savings that could have gone for retirement are being used to fund living expenses. The net result is that the generations that followed the baby boomers into the workforce tend to have fewer years of full-time employment. This restricts a family's ability to save for retirement.

Ongoing Government Financial Stress - Massive government debt has become the norm and even periods of strong economic activity have not led to a reduction in our accumulated debt. Although some believe the debt should be repaid, politicians understand the public does not want reduced services.

Fast forward a couple of decades when baby boomers are hitting retirement homes in massive numbers. In addition to providing government services, defense spending, infrastructure investments, debt repayment (kidding) and the like, can we afford to provide seniors with the services they require? We need more beds, personal support workers and medical services at a time when our accumulated debt continues to grow. Although there are many wealthy retirees who can fund their final years, we will have millions who lack the resources to pay for the care they require.

> **Then** - Although there were deficits during the boomer's era, there was sufficient tax revenue to fund seniors' pension and health care needs.

> **Now** - It is rare to find a government that can balance the books on an annual basis and there is no discussion of eliminating the accumulated debt. Paying for the boomer's end of life expenses will create an incredible burden on the next generation.

Contraction of Business Locations - The rapid expansion of the economy after the Second World War resulted in companies having branches, manufacturing facilities, sales offices and processing plants spread across the country. Most small towns had at least one major employer. This resulted in a source of jobs for high school graduates and reasonably priced homes. As employment in the manufacturing sector declined, many plants were closed. Technology introduced a level of central control and it was not necessary for companies to have offices in the cities they served. If a company needed to expand capacity, it was often more cost effective to build a new one rather than refurbish an old facility. The small towns across the country were often ignored as companies considered expansion options.

This contraction of business locations left many small communities hurting. In the past, high school graduates from these small towns had employment opportunities without leaving home. Currently, many leave their community to pursue higher education or find suitable employment.

> **Then** - Many small towns had a major employer that could provide a middle-class lifestyle to semi-skilled local residents.

> **Now** - Many communities feel left behind in today's economy. There are too few jobs that pay a sufficient salary to allow families to finance their retirement. Upgrading skills and moving to a larger community is often the pathway to suitable employment, but many families are reluctant to move in search of a better life.

Introduction of a Gig Economy - A gig economy refers to employers achieving flexibility and cost savings by using part-time and contract staff, rather than full-time employees. For those who are unable to achieve the status of a full-time employee, it means working at lower rates of pay, minimal benefits and a lack of a pension plan. Those caught in this lifestyle often defer buying a house and starting a family. Baby boomers left school and stepped into full-time jobs, but that transition can no longer be taken for granted. There may be an extended period of time between graduation and full-time employment. Unfortunately for many workers, it appears the gig economy is part of the new normal.

From the employer's perspective, fewer full-time employees is becoming the preferred business model, especially for major projects. They can hire the skills they need and when the job is finished, individuals take their skill set elsewhere. There is less of a need to invest in training since the individuals with the necessary skills can be hired on a short-term basis. Although this type of work may be preferable to some individuals, such as those winding down their career, it is challenging to be an active participant in the gig economy and save for retirement. No pensions, periods of unemployment and lack of certainty concerning next year's income is not the norm of a workplace enjoyed by their parents.

> **Then** - After graduation, individuals found a job and it was commonplace to only work for one or two employers over an entire career. Defined benefits pensions were offered by most large companies.

> **Now** - Employers utilize contract workers and part-time staff as a low-cost alternative to full-time employees. Individuals entering the workforce may work for numerous employers throughout their career. This restricts the ability of individuals to earn pension credits.

The Walmart Job Paradox

Working families want fair paying jobs and inexpensive products sold by Walmart, many of which are imported from Asia. Is this a conflict? If the products sold by Walmart were made in North America, more workers would have jobs, but the goods sold by the company would be more expensive. Is paying more for a product, the price we have to pay to keep manufacturing jobs from moving overseas? Simplistically, the question could be asked whether we want well-paying manufacturing jobs or lower prices offered by imported products. Although this may seem at first blush like a thought-provoking question, it misses the point in today's economy. If these products were produced in North America, it would not result in a significant increase in the number of semi-skilled workers employed. New manufacturing facilities utilize robotics, artificial intelligence and highly skilled workers. The production may return home, but the jobs will not follow.

Bottom Line - Retirement is financed by employer and government pensions, plus our ability to self-fund retirement. Membership in defined benefit pensions is declining, while fewer employers offer a pension plan of any type. Reduced pension income means more families must self-finance retirement. The nature of work has changed and many families use their earnings to pay for living expenses and there is little left over to fund retirement. That leaves government pensions as a primary source of income for many families and that is dreadfully inadequate.

PART FOUR

GOVERNMENT'S ROLE

CHAPTER FOURTEEN

GOVERNMENT POLICY OPTIONS

The goal is not to live forever,
but to create something that does.

Government spending has a significant impact on the quality of life enjoyed by seniors. As the boomers enter retirement in record numbers, seniors will make up an increasing percentage of the population which will result in a greater demand for government-funded services. In most western countries, those sixty-five and older constitute about 16% of the population and this will rise to about 25% in the year 2050. An aging population will result in increased spending on health care, community support workers and nursing home accommodation. The cost to care for this segment of the population will be very large, especially when many families lack the financial resources to be self-sufficient.

This raises the question whether governments will prioritize spending on seniors and will the increased expenditures result in higher taxes or larger deficits? If governments are unable or unwilling to pay these costs, options include rationing services or requiring higher-income families to be responsible for a larger share of their costs. The policy issues our government must address include:

- At what age should individuals be eligible to receive government pensions?

- A large number of retirees will rely on government assistance as their primary source of income. Is it time to consider a guaranteed annual income for seniors?

- Can the government afford to pay the entire cost of seniors' health care? Should coverage include prescriptions, dental care, mobility equipment, home care and mental health counseling?

- How should society resolve the issue of able-bodied people who refuse to perform low paying or undesirable work? Those who do not work during a significant portion of their adult life, have almost no chance of self-funding retirement.

- Should governments guarantee workers' pensions in case of employer bankruptcies?

The Age for Pension Eligibility

Back in the day, many men worked in physically demanding jobs and retired when their bodies started to wear down. A lack of private pension and minimal savings resulted in government pensions becoming their primary source of income. However, as the boomers approached retirement, a fixed retirement date become more complex as financial inequality continued to widen. Boomers with personal wealth or excellent pensions were often able to retire before the age of sixty and government pensions only served to supplement their retirement income. However, a significant portion of the population cannot afford to retire and are unable to find meaningful work. As a result, they are dependent on the government to pay the bills. The problem is further compounded as individuals who did not work for an extended period of their adult life and survived on welfare, disability payments or "off-book" income do not qualify for full government pensions.

At what age should an individual qualify for a government pension? This issue is complicated as there are two distinct worlds of retirees. There is one group that requires government pensions to pay the bills, i.e., the have-nots. They retired with a lack of savings and no pension income. Regardless of their work history, they have arrived in retirement and are unable to pay their living expenses without government assistance. This group needs access to pensions as soon as possible. The other world is the haves who are financially secure and pensions provide additional income, that is nice to have but not necessary to sustain their lifestyle. If they did not receive their pension until age seventy, it would not be a major hardship. It is a challenge to balance these two worlds. It is further complicated as higher income individuals have paid into the pension throughout their working careers, while lower-income families have contributed significantly less. Depending upon one's political perspective, this is either a major issue or irrelevant.

Our cash-strapped government faces a number of options. They can increase the financial viability of pensions by delaying the date that individuals qualify to receive benefits. For example, if the age was seventy, recipients would have fewer years to receive benefits and would extend the number of years they pay into the retirement plans. Politicians must balance the actuarial recommendations with political considerations. The bottom line is individuals that require a greater level of assistance need access to their pensions at an earlier age, whereas the more financially secure can afford to defer the start date. As a result, one solution does not fit all seniors.

Guaranteed Annual Income for Seniors

The idea of some type of guaranteed annual income has gained traction in Europe but maybe its time has arrived in North America as a solution to poverty among seniors. When individuals reach an age when work is not an option, such as age seventy, is it possible to provide a basic income that ensures they stay above the poverty line? There are a number of common objections to any type of guaranteed annual income plan. They range from its cost to philosophical objections as it is a form of socialism, but that may be the price to be paid to eliminate poverty among seniors. If we had a world with free medical services, a guaranteed level of income and subsidized retirement homes for those who require assistance, we would have taken a major step to eliminate the financial component of retirement hell. Whether or not we implement a guaranteed annual income or similar type of funding, the bottom line is that many seniors' lifestyle will be financed by the government.

Health Care and Seniors

A financially secure retirement requires both income and access to health care services. The level and quality of health care are dependent on where individuals reside and their income level. Countries in North America and Western Europe have three different models of care. The system used in the United States is private health care supplemented by Medicare and Medicaid for the elderly and the poor. Canada has a publicly funded universal health care system, while Europe tends to use a combined public-private system.

The structure and funding of health care is a settled issue in most countries with the exception of the United States. They have world-class care for those with appropriate insurance coverage, but as a country, they struggle to ensure all citizens receive the care they require on a timely basis. America does not appear to have an appetite to copy best practices from other western countries as their systems are considered to be a form of socialism. The term socialist to many Americans is like the term cooties to a child. They are not sure what it is, but it must be bad.

Although, the Canadian health care system is classed as a public system; it is the best of all worlds for wealthy or connected individuals. In theory, the health care is funded by the tax system and if a person requires cancer treatment and related surgeries, there are no out of pocket costs. However, for many hospital procedures, wait times are a significant issue. Seniors who need hip or knee replacement surgery may have to wait over twelve months to have the procedure completed. However, for individuals that have connections, it is possible to move to the front of the line. A doctor's spouse will probably receive more timely treatment, than your next-door neighbor. One doctor tells the story of the hypocrisy of many Canadian politicians. Although they publicly sing the praises of the universal health care system, but when they have a friend or family member who requires medical services, they often pressure doctors to let the patient jump the line and receive immediate attention.

Although Canadian politicians claim it is a public system, there is an exception for the wealthy. They can gain access to a large private health system care by crossing the border and receiving care in the United States. If there is a fifteen-month backlog for a certain operation in Canada, a call can be made to facilities such as the Cleveland or Mayo Clinics and the problem of wait times will disappear. These world-class American hospitals have set up systems to help Canadian residents receive medical assistance in the United States. The patient will pay a significant fee for these services, but if they want immediate help, it is available. For example, an elderly lady in Canada needed knee replacement surgery and was advised that the wait time for the operation would be approximately fifteen months. This was unacceptable to her husband who believes she may only have a few more years of mobility and it made no sense a spend a significant portion of her remaining years in pain with restricted motion. A call was made to a large American hospital, an appointment was booked and the surgery was scheduled for the next week. No doubt there was a significant financial hit, but it was considered a reduction in their children's legacy and both parents were fine with that outcome.

Should health care be a right? You can bet you damn ass it is and this seems to be a settled question throughout Western society, with one notable exception. A fundamental requirement to avoid retirement hell is access to health care. A person with cancer must receive the necessary treatment in a timely fashion regardless of income or ability to pay. There is not unanimous support for the foregoing statement, but those who oppose this concept tend to have access to health care for themselves and their family. Given the massive cost and the number of patients that will be impacted as baby boomers flood the system, will this result in constraints being imposed on our health care system? The needs of the patients may exceed the capacity of the system to deliver the necessary services. Difficult questions must be addressed to determine the level of services to be provided. Governments may be forced to draw a line in the sand based on the amount of funding they are prepared to dedicate to health care. Not only will this line change over time, but there will be sharp disagreements as to what should be covered. Issues may include:

- Do we supply wheelchairs or motorized carts for those requiring assistance with mobility?
- Should our health care system, include services for seniors who are struggling with mental health issues.
- Do we cover the cost of high-cost prescriptions when cheaper alternatives are not available? For example, although these are not drugs aimed specifically at seniors, Glybera treats familial lipoprotein lipase deficiency and costs over a million dollars per annum. Soliris costs just under $450,000 and treats paroxysmal nocturnal

hemoglobinuria. These are rare diseases, but prescriptions are cost prohibitive. Some drugs are expensive because they treat a small base of patients, while some companies charge what the market will bear and some gouge because they can.

- Should we cover gender reassignment surgery for a ninety-one-year-old senior who believes he has lived in the wrong body for too many years?
- Is there any age an individual should no longer qualify for cancer care or hip replacement surgery?
- We need a vast number of beds and support workers as the boomers hit retirement homes. Should governments be in the business of providing accommodation to seniors or should it be outsourced to the private sector?
- Should unlimited dental care be included in the services provided?
- Will these services be free to all seniors or will the ability to pay be considered? Perhaps there will be deductible for those over a certain income level.

Low Wage Jobs

If a person chooses not to work for any reason, there is normally some form of welfare or social assistance to ensure the individual does not starve. Many individuals do not suffer a significant loss of income by not working and collecting pogey or disability payments as compared to having a part-time job at minimum wage. Many jobs would go unfilled if the work was not performed by newcomers to our country. Many farmers are allowed to bring in guest workers to pick the crops, as the locals are not interested in this back-breaking work. Certain industries offer low pay and less than ideal working conditions. Examples would include fish and meat processing, agriculture, workers in the hospitality industry and those who care for our elderly population. These jobs are often filled by newcomers to the country. This is not a slight at these workers as they are prepared to do the work that many native-born workers shun.

We have allowed a situation to arise where when given a choice between working and collecting social assistance; it may make economic sense for certain individuals not to work. A young single mother may choose not to work as she does not have access to affordable daycare. A young man who has the choice of working in a fish processing plant for slightly more than minimum wage or collecting some form of government assistance may believe that he made a rational economic decision by staying at home.

Working not only provides a paycheck, but there is a social benefit of getting out in the world and being a part of society. Can we change the equation, so there is an advantage by working, rather than choosing social assistance or disability? The number of years in the workforce has an impact on an individual's retirement income. The amount of government pensions is based on career earnings. In addition to the value of contributing to society rather than being a "taker," there can be an incredible amount of personal growth by holding a job. There is a socialization process that can be invaluable to those that get out of bed and go to work, but the advantages are often not recognized by those who stay home.

As a society, we have tried various solutions from workfare to time limits on welfare, but we are not prepared to let people starve, especially if there are children involved. One potential solution is a large refundable tax credit for low-income individuals. These credits can provide an incentive for lower income employment.

Pension Guarantees - If a company offers a defined benefit pension plan and becomes bankrupt, both current employees and retirees may lose a significant portion of their pension income. In such cases, does the government have a role in protecting the workers? It is cost prohibitive to finance the entire shortfall, but they could make employees preferred creditors in bankruptcy proceedings. This would ensure their claims are ranked higher than other creditors. Another option is the introduction of tighter rules on pension contributions to better manage unfunded liabilities.

If an insurance company is paying a retirement annuity and goes bankrupt, the seniors who were the recipients of the payments may find their financial security has been devastated. The risks could be reduced by increased regulation to ensure the financial viability of the payor, but increased government regulations are falling out of favor in certain jurisdictions.

Bottom Line – Governments have lived beyond their means for years and the day of reckoning may come if they cannot afford to provide seniors with the necessaries of life. Government policies impact our lifestyle in retirement. The key concern is whether our financially stressed government can afford the various expenses of health care, pensions and funding retirement homes. From a health care perspective, will the government be able to pay all of a senior's medical expenses or will the patient be expected to pay a portion of the cost? When baby boomers start to flood into retirement homes, will we have sufficient beds, support workers and medical services to care for this generation? It appears that a significant portion of the population will rely on government pensions to pay their bills. If the government's objective is to eliminate senior poverty, the cost may exceed their ability to pay without causing extreme financial stress in the economy.

CHAPTER FIFTEEN

A BIPOLAR CHAPTER

Why is confidence quiet, while insecurity is loud?

Note - This first part of this chapter argues in support of government mandated affirmative action to eliminate age bias and discrimination against older workers. Part two is unkind to diversity programs and argues it is a form of legislatively supported discrimination. This is based on the view that discrimination is wrong regardless of any motivation to correct past injustices. The hypocrisy of trying to blow and suck at the same time is not lost on the author. Affirmative action attempts to assist various groups in our society that have suffered some form of discrimination in the past and therefore are under-represented at various jobs and pay levels. Women and minorities were the primary beneficiaries of these policies. However, many older workers are either underemployed or cannot find work since employers favor younger workers. This is a form of discrimination which raises the question whether governments should apply affirmative action programs to assist older workers.

Part One - Ageism

In order to reduce age-based discrimination, governments have introduced legislation such as the end of mandatory retirement for certain jobs. However, these laws tend to ensure those who are currently employed maintain their job but offers little hope to those that are unemployed. Many people over the age of fifty have lost their job and are having trouble finding full-time employment at a comparable salary. This is a peak earning period and the elimination of a well-paying job can decimate a family's plan for retirement.

In prior decades, when discrimination against women and minorities was rampant in society, governments became involved when it was clear that employers were not making progress at an acceptable pace. As a result, we had various affirmative action programs that alleviated much of the problem. Currently, many older workers are subject to age-based discrimination and governments do not appear to be inclined to use legislative remedies to ease this problem for older workers.

When companies hire new employees, workers between the age of 50 and 65 are significantly underrepresented. There are a plethora of reasons why companies prefer younger workers. There is no issue that older workers have a responsibility to upgrade their skills to ensure they can perform the functions that companies require. Unfortunately, the older employee's maturity, experience and work ethic are discounted in the hiring process.

Employers believe they have legitimate reasons to favor younger workers, but if the same logic applied to a refusal to hire women or gays, there would an outcry and possible legal consequences. Ask a hiring manager why he prefers to hire younger staff over more seasoned employees and typical responses include - more current on technology, salary expectations are more reasonable or perhaps because of their age they are perceived to be more flexible to adapt to a new job situation. Ask a similar philosophical question to a hiring manager as to why he prefers white employees over visible minorities and you will be told the question is beyond offensive and would not be dignified with a response.

Even if employers can get past their stereotypes of older workers as being outdated on technology and stuck in their ways, older employees may have to adjust their expectations. They must be prepared to have a boss who is younger than their children, temper their salary expectations and understand their age and experience may be seen as negatives by their co-workers. Many government departments have diversity targets for management positions and perhaps the time has come to consider older workers who are underemployed or without a job even if they are white males. If that happens, the pendulum would have swung back in the other direction as middle-aged white males were a group that had previously been negatively impacted by affirmative action programs.

Discrimination against older workers does exist, but we should not expect any government action on this issue. The right side of the political spectrum tends to be against affirmative action. The supporters on the left will never give an advantage to older white males if it restricts opportunities for any of the other groups in society that were repressed in the past, such as women, minorities or members of the LGBT community. Companies are discriminating against older workers, but should the government have a role in fixing the issue? Such a program would make a world of difference for those that are attempting to save for retirement, but as for any action that would benefit white males from working families, do not hold your breath.

Perhaps the most succinct perspective is that ageism does not exist unless you are looking for a job or a date.

Part Two - Affirmative Action

Once the boomers had been in the workforce for a few decades, it became clear that not everyone was sharing in the opportunities. Most senior positions were filled by white men and on average males were paid a higher salary than females. As women and minorities entered the job market, they were not only underrepresented and underpaid in many jobs, but many businesses did not appear to recognize the problem or take the necessary steps to address the issue. As a result, governments and the courts became involved. Thus, we entered the world of mandatory diversity, also known as affirmative action. It was designed to eliminate inequities, remove structural barriers and end systemic discrimination. We were introduced to terms such as glass ceiling, quotas, token hiring and reverse discrimination. It impacted businesses, government, universities and anywhere that smelled of the old boy's network, other than religious organizations which are still the gold standard for gender bias.

Diversity programs were very controversial and it was painful for many companies and white males. There were winners and losers, but many females and minorities owe their success to affirmative action programs and pay equity. However, there was a dark side as many were passed over for promotion or not hired simply because they were white or male. Although many under-qualified people received jobs they did not deserve and performed poorly, there are also incredible success stories of females and minorities who never had an opportunity, so when they got a chance to shine, shine they did. As women and minorities graduated university in record numbers and started to advance through corporations and universities, these programs may become less important.

Despite the many positives that resulted from governments legislating diversity initiatives, there were also many losers. Large companies hired and promoted to meet government-imposed targets, but for employees that did not meet the requirements of the job, some companies would address the issue, while other would identify their problem children and shuffle them to positions where they could do minimal damage. As a private sector executive remarked, "Thank God for human resource departments." A young lady could be a secretary one week and a human resource manager the next. It is rare for large companies to find an HR department that has a majority of males. (Was that too subtle?) In certain government positions, diversity was considered more important than competence and there are managers that should thank the lucky stars for these programs. They received their jobs because of diversity targets, are inept, but have job security. In most cases, their co-workers understand, senior managers are aware and customers just shake their head, yet many of these managers strut around as if they earned their position.

Besides ageism, there are still a number of occupations that do not have appropriate gender representation, but the government has been slow to act. Examples would include grade three teachers, nurses and dental hygienists. If not for diversity, how will men have a chance to compete in these fields? It appears society is concerned about lack of female graduates in engineering and technology, but not so much with the lack of men in nursing and veterinarian sciences. Educational inequality will continue to work against men and any attempt to use affirmative action strategies to increase male enrollment or put restrictions on females seems to be a non-starter.

Should a company be allowed to hire the most qualified candidates, even if it results in employee representation that does not mirror the makeup of society? For the sake of argument, let's assume there are neither systemic impediments nor subtle forms of discrimination to keep everyone from qualifying. If a large law firm had twenty partners who were all white males, many would find this unacceptable, even if the firm honestly believed they hired the best of the best and they just happened to be white males. Some organizations are allowed to hire the most qualified candidate and disregard diversity. For example:

- NBA teams, especially starting players seem to lack white athletes.

- Starting cornerbacks in the NFL tend to exclude white football players.
- Can anyone remember that last time a white person competed for the U.S. Olympic team in the 4 X 100 relay?

Are these examples of discrimination or are the most qualified and deserving athletes getting their rightful job? These teams do not represent the makeup of society, yet we are prepared to live with this anomaly since certain jobs must have the most qualified candidates. Most would agree that hiring the best of the best when it comes to athletics, but it is not necessarily a principle that should be applied to government and business. Many people do not support opportunities that were awarded because of diversity. If less qualified minorities were admitted to a university to fill a quota system, many considered this offensive. It was seen as a type of reverse discrimination, as white males were denied access, even though they had superior qualifications. If current trends continue, and more university spots are filled by women, we may require a quota system to ensure white men are properly represented in post-secondary institutions. Since many of the most qualified students may be women and Asians, how else can we make room for underperforming men at our post-secondary institutions?

Despite the success of diversity programs in achieving their goals, some groups are still underrepresented, some legitimately and others not so much. There are flaws in the theory of diversity, but it is seldom challenged since underrepresentation of minorities and females must be wrong. Flaws in diversity theory include:

Theory - An organization's makeup should reflect the community in which they are situated.

Flaw - If there is no systemic discrimination, an organization's makeup should reflect the hiring pool from which candidates are selected, rather than the community as a whole. The higher the skill level, the less likely the hiring pool will reflect the community. For example, if a company wants to hire ten scientists who are completing their thesis, they may have a different ethnic makeup than shoppers at the local Walmart. If a police department believes they are underrepresented by openly gay men, they can try to target this group, but they may have a problem. If candidates that are hired as police officers must complete some type of police foundations or a basic training course prior to being hired and if openly gay men do not register in these basic courses, it can difficult to find suitable candidates. This does not appear to be an issue with female officers. Even if a police department is underrepresented by heterosexual female officers, there will be no hue and cry to ensure there is proper proportional representation in the force.

Theory - By having the various ethnicities that mirror society working for an organization, they can speak for and represent their community.

Flaw - All workers bring a sum of their experiences to the job. There is no issue that different ethnic or gender backgrounds can bring fresh perspectives. However, it is wrong to expect employees to be representatives of their race or culture. Could you imagine telling a young man who was just hired that he is expected to bring the white man's perspective to the discussion? Many would consider that offensive.

Theory - Diversity programs use legislation to correct past injustices.

Flaw - Discrimination is wrong, regardless of the reason. Period.

If you are a male who is underemployed with a horrible sex life, have you considered ditching your gonads, embracing your feminine side and seek opportunities as a transgender person? This group is underrepresented in most business and government offices. (Note - The previous comment was meant to be tongue in cheek so do not take this suggestion literally and make an appointment with a surgeon.)

Consider the story of a young man who lived on a reservation outside of my city. We had not been in contact for about three years. When we met by chance, he provided an update on his life. He was enrolled in a community college and taking business courses. He was not troubled by his low marks and made the following statement - "My grades are poor, but I will be the highest paid graduate in my class. I am an Indian with a college degree and employers will fight each other to hire me." Is this a story to celebrate or should it make us sad?

The diversity gravy train is coming to an end as many employers have addressed the structural problems that resulted in females and minorities being underrepresented. In the future, fewer will be hired or receive promotions based on genitalia or skin pigmentation. However, as for the discrimination facing older workers, it continues to be a problem that is not being addressed.

Bottom Line - The color of your skin and sexual orientation tells nothing of a person's character. In a just society, these factors should not result in any disadvantage, nor be the basis of any opportunities.

PART FIVE

ETHICS

CHAPTER SIXTEEN

ETHICS AND ECONOMIC SUCCESS

Perfection is the enemy of good.

The next few chapters may seem out of place in a book about avoiding the dark underbelly of retirement. However, ethics can be a significant contributor to a financially secure retirement on two distinct levels - individual and the strength of our economy. Ethical people are more likely to have a successful career than those that are dishonest or unprincipled. The ethically challenged often have their careers fall apart as a consequence of some inappropriate action. Reading this or any other book will not result in individuals acting in a more responsible manner, but it is possible to establish ethical norms that will increase the likelihood of appropriate behavior within a person's span of control. This may include a business or groups of individuals such as employees or family members.

There are various academic studies on corruption and its impact on the economy and the middle class. It results in increased income inequality, slower economic growth, wasteful government spending, tax avoidance and the growth of an underground economy. Corruption weakens the middle class and will restrict some families ability to fund their retirement.

Growing up in a small Ontario town, the local arena was the hub of our winter activity. Although a few of my heroes made it to the NHL (Gary Doak, Al Dewsbury, Larry Jeffrey and Jack Price), most kids played for the enjoyment of the game. In the old barn where the games were played, there was a press box that had a poem written on the front boards. The last lines were "he marks not that you won or lost, but how you played the game." There was a day when sportsmanship was more important than winning. It was a philosophy that parents taught their children, but it was not clear if they really believed the advice or it was just another feel-good Santa Claus story.

In our daily lives, most of are inclined to do the right thing and not break the law. However, we live in a world of big money and concentrated power and playing fair has taken a back seat to winning. It appears in the hardball worlds of politics and business that ethical standards have devolved through a four-part process:

Stage One -The age of innocence

Doing the right thing and playing by the rules is more important than winning.

Stage Two - The era of competitiveness

The goal is to win but do it fair and square.

Stage Three - Mean spirited victories

The goal is to win by any means. Take no prisoners, however, ensure you do not run afoul of the law.

Stage Four - A world of lawyers in a post-truth society

Winning is the only option and if the law is broken, ensure you are not convicted.

Even though most people in the world of business are ethical and honest, it has become more common to achieve financial gain or success by playing outside the rules. Many people are coming face to face with the difficult ethical dilemma of why should they play by the rules if their competitors do not? Breaking the rules and not suffering a penalty can open new avenues of greed. Most people want to play by the rules and expect the government to ensure the playing field is level. The police can enforce the rules of crimes against people and property, but financial fraud that can eliminate a family's savings and retirement funds often lacks criminal convictions and the recovery of missing funds.

Corruption is a contributor to income inequality and results in working families losing their jobs, investments and retirement savings. Consider the following examples:

- The financial crisis of 2008 was caused by shenanigans which resulted from deregulation in the banking industry. We were introduced to liar loans, subprime mortgages and the bankruptcy of Lehman Brothers. The value of investments was reduced by over two trillion dollars, which resulted in many families forced to delay their retirement. The crisis resulted in the loss of jobs, a decline in housing prices and foreclosures which resulted in families being kicked out of their homes. Credit was difficult to obtain and many companies could not receive the necessary financing and businesses collapsed. Despite these outrageous practices, no one went to jail. Some companies were convicted, but that resulted in corporate fines, rather than jail terms.

- Corruption in society reduces the taxes collected by governments, so honest taxpayers are obligated to pay their fair share, plus a little bit more. If there is a perception of corruption in a country, this increases the likelihood of a growing underground economy.

- If we have a corrupt government, opportunities are not available to everyone. Those with political connections will be rewarded and governments will pay more for certain projects while many companies will not have a legitimate chance to procure the business.

There has been a reduction of ethical standards in recent years. There was a day when there was an expectation of consequences for inappropriate decisions. We understand that advertising contains puffery, politicians talk out of both sides of their mouth but who could have imagined a scenario that the leader of a country would lie on a regular basis and this would not be an issue with his core supporters? There has always been a sense of entitlement among the wealthy, but that trait has become common in many of our children. We currently live in a world where culprits are able to justify their actions by the unfortunate circumstances of their birth. Many are able to avoid the consequences of their actions if they are wealthy, well-connected, a great athlete or protected by unions or professional organizations. Much of the malfeasance in society could be eliminated if we implemented a code of honor such as the one used at West Point of the FBI. The West Point rule is straightforward - "a cadet will not lie, cheat, steal, or tolerate those who do." If the action of an FBI employee is being investigated internally, the lack of truthfulness is an offense punishable by being fired. Could you imagine if governments, judicial organizations and large companies had a code of conduct that included fireable offenses? If you break the rules, you lose your job. This old-school view of ethics is out of fashion and it appears dishonesty has become more acceptable in our society. Power, wealth, access to top-shelf legal counsel and membership in certain organizations are able to shield many individuals who should be fired, jailed or found guilty of various offenses. It is doubtful if this ethical slippage can be reversed. The key to eliminating corruption in society is having consequences for those who break the rules. If this means putting a bunch of rich white guys with political connections in prison, is that all bad?

Ethics Prejudice and Tribalism

Tribalism and prejudice appear to be a component of our character. Most people have the ability to keep their dark thoughts hidden away, but it is naïve to believe these feelings do not exist. Consider the following example. Mr. Reid is a sales rep that travels the world for his employer. While walking down a busy street in Manhattan, he crosses paths with Mr. Smith who is an incredibly average, middle-aged, slightly overweight white man hurrying to his next meeting. Does our sales rep make eye contact or acknowledge this stranger on the street? Since they have never met, the street is packed and everyone is going about their business, there is no reason to notice, acknowledge or speak to Mr. Smith. He is just a face in the crowd and there is no reason to interact.

Fast forward one year and Mr. Reid is working in Kano Nigeria, a city of approximately three million people. The rep has been in the city for five days and has not seen another white face since his arrival. On the final day of the trip, the sales rep is walking down a busy street and Mr. Smith our average, middle-aged, slightly overweight white man that was ignored in Manhattan is walking towards him in Kano. Is there any doubt they would each acknowledge the only white person they have both seen in a week? Is there a reason other than race that resulted in the two white men acknowledging each other?

Tribalism and prejudice may run deep and even though we wished these feelings did not exist, a prudent people will neither share their views nor act upon them.

Bottom Line - There is a higher probability of financial success for men and women of uncompromising character.

They are referred to as "boy scouts" or "straight arrows" and are strong enough to forego short-term advantages and are able to define themselves by their strength of character. An individual who has a reputation for honesty and uncompromising integrity will have opportunities for success that are not available to others. If we could just do the right thing and quit pretending that we are smart enough to fool our peers, we may discover opportunities that we never knew existed. A reduction in corruption, especially as it applies to banking and investment fraud, will strengthen the middle class and safeguard the savings of working families.

There are things in life that we know in our heart to be true but are difficult to prove. I believe people of integrity and character will not only be more successful in their career, but they make the best friends, spouses and co-workers. I know it to be true, but it is difficult to prove.

CHAPTER SEVENTEEN

TERMINOLOGY

Inside of me, there are two dogs. One is mean and evil and the other is good and they fight each other all the time. The one who wins is the one I feed the most.

Sitting Bull

Throughout my journey in the corporate world, I came into contact with many successful people from working families. What sets these individuals apart from their peers? In addition to being very good at their job, they shared two traits - an incredible work ethic and a strong moral compass.

The importance of ethics may sound like a statement of the obvious, but to be successful one must have the opportunity and it is commonly attained by individuals who can be trusted. Many intelligent, but ethically challenged people, lost their jobs or had their career stalled when it was discovered they were dishonest. Unfortunately, many believe they are so smart and cunning that they can lie and deceive their peers and their unethical behavior goes unnoticed. They assume they are smarter than their co-workers and like most fools, they overestimate their ability to behave badly and avoid the consequences. This is not to suggest that the ethically challenged have not been successful, but in most cases, the success does not last until retirement.

Terminology

The terms morals, ethics and integrity have distinct meanings, but in general parlance, these terms are often used interchangeably.

Morals – These are the principles we use to determine what is right and wrong. It is a code that guides an individual's behavior. However, morality is not a concept on which people agree. For example, some may find abortion to be immoral, while others find it a choice that should be available to all women. There was a time if a woman was not a virgin on her wedding night she was considered immoral. Morals evolve over time and society tends to become more tolerant of those who see the world in a different way. Morality can be influenced by religion and culture. Most employers do not care about their employee's sense of morality unless it causes some level of embarrassment for the organization. There are exceptions such as the Catholic Church. If the goal is to become a priest, a young man's sense of morality must mirror that of the Church, or a dream of the priesthood may vanish. However, if individuals were applying for a position at a top technology company, their views on abortion, capital punishment and politics may never enter into the hiring decision.

Ethics – It is a code of behavior for a group or organization. Members of the group are expected to follow certain rules, or there will be consequences. In the case of corporations, the code of ethics may be written or implied. It is easy to understand the importance of ethical standards to a professional association or a large corporation, but codes exist everywhere, including criminal organizations. If individuals joined an outlaw biker gang, they would soon appreciate there is a code of conduct for members just as employees of a multinational company have rules that define expected behavior. In the case of a biker group, new members learn the rules and expectations very quickly.

They may not be written down but breaking the code can result in swift and severe consequences. I have no knowledge of biker organizations or how they operate, but my sense is that if a new member invites his brother-in-law to a bash and does not inform his fellow club members that his guest is an undercover police officer there would be consequences. Employees will bring their individual morality to a job, which is normally irrelevant in the workplace, while an organization will impose its own code of ethics on its members.

Integrity - Personal ethics and integrity can be used interchangeably. For individuals, there are two types of ethical behavior - ethics of conviction and situational ethics. Ethics of conviction means doing the right thing regardless of the consequences. If it means reporting their child to the authorities for a criminal code violation, they will take the necessary steps because they believe it is the right thing to do. They often pay the price for taking bold stands, but they define themselves by their principles. Such individuals are great employees and friends but can be a pain in the butt to deal with when they stand on their principles and seem unwilling to compromise. Would you want friends of such high ethical standards that under no circumstances would they tell a lie to keep you out of trouble? Situational ethics takes a pragmatic approach and weighs the negative consequences of doing the right thing, the possibility of getting caught and the individuals involved. For example, many people would throw their principles out the window and would do whatever is necessary to protect a family member. For many people, ethical responses are a calculation, rather than acting on principles that are etched in stone.

Integrity is a part of individual's personality that demands a person do the right thing, be honest, fair and truthful. It is a high standard that is expected of our spouse, children, bosses and co-workers. It is straightforward to understand the concept of integrity, but it is difficult to measure, as most people will present a face to the world that suggests that they are as honest as the day is long. People with integrity will do the right thing because of their personal values, rather than to avoid a penalty even if it means giving up a financial advantage. Moral compass is a term used to gauge an individual's ability to distinguish right and wrong and then act accordingly.

There are a number of factors that make integrity a complex issue:

- With the possible exception of some of our mothers, no one is perfect. We may grow in character and make fewer mistakes as we age, but perfection is not a reasonable expectation.
- One can behave properly in some aspects of life but have a hidden flaw that is a part of their character. A man who appears to be a person of outstanding character and would not steal under any circumstances but will screw around on his wife. He could be a plumber or a president.
- Ethics are often situational. If there a possible financial or sexual advantage to be achieved, inappropriate decisions may follow. Decisions may be made based on the circumstances of the moment, including the possibility of getting caught, rather than relying on principles that are cast in stone.

The threat of adverse consequences can pressure individuals to behave in a manner that appears inconsistent with their character. A person conscripted into the army of some despot may carry out horrific acts and justify the behavior as only following orders. Sales reps that are paid on commission may distort the truth as they attempt to sell products that are a poor choice for the customer. In some cases, this is puffery, while other times it is outright fraud. Academic studies, such as the famous Stanford Prison Experiment, indicate that ordinary individuals are capable of bad behavior when given a level of power and are coerced to behave inappropriately. This study indicates that a person's response might be the result of the situation encountered, rather than a component of their personality. It suggests that character is something that can be molded or manipulated a lot easier than we might expect.

Integrity is more than following rules; it is living a life based on values. Our actions are guided by these values and our friends and family have come to expect we will act according to these principles. As a society, we cannot agree on many issues or even form a consensus between right and wrong. Values have been nourished throughout our lives by parents, teachers and our conscience. From a workforce perspective, the most important values a person may possess are honesty, work ethic and treating others in a respectful manner. In other words, these are the values that were established by the greatest generation when their efforts laid the foundation for the middle class. The greatest generation refers to those who were born between 1900 and 1925. This is not to suggest that this generation was the ideal role model for those who followed. Perhaps their greatest strength was their work ethic that was not impaired by a sense of entitlement which became embedded in many of their grandchildren. As a generation, perhaps their greatest weakness was the insensitivity shown to minorities and people who were different than them.

Ethics and the Law - Following the law does not necessarily imply one is acting ethically. Our laws tend to be consistent with the mores of society. However, following the law does not imply the behavior is ethical, rather it means that there will be no consequences for such actions. There was a day when slavery was legal, women could not vote and minorities faced horrific discrimination. Look around the world and there are numerous examples of laws that are wrong. Many protests and cries for social justice are aimed at laws that some people believe are inconsistent with the values of our country.

Bottom Line - We are imperfect creatures, but if we can convince ourselves that it is in our long-term best interests to do the right thing and forego short-term gains, there is usually a payoff in our careers and relationships. Unethical behavior restricts an individual's ability to take advantage of opportunities, while corruption ensures the playing field is not level. If individuals are perceived as unethical, they will have fewer opportunities than would otherwise be available. Individuals with criminal records may have trouble finding employment, whereas those who are ethically challenged may struggle to keep their current job.

CHAPTER EIGHTEEN

CREATING AN ETHICAL ENVIRONMENT

If you want to help criminals, promote bad behavior and thwart justice, never be a snitch.

Within an individual's span of control, such as family, business or group of employees, it is possible to create a culture where proper behavior is expected and inappropriate actions can be minimized. Since ethical behavior is often situational, the objective is to build an environment where appropriate actions are the norm.

If an individual is a member of a group where positive behavior is rewarded and unethical actions are punished, people of strong character will thrive. The most important player in the ethics dynamic is the individual at the top of the food chain, be it a parent, manager, or CEO. There are two styles of leadership as it relates to ethics and they are known as "tone at the top" and "rank has its privileges." The "tone at the top" style means that the leader's behavior will set the standard for the organization. If the leader behaves ethically and sets it as an expectation, it becomes a strong inducement for others to act appropriately. Such conduct is further reinforced if there are punishments for unethical behavior that are applied swiftly without regard to the title or position of the offender. There is a negative corollary of this style. If the leader lies, steals and cheats, will those that report to him act differently? For example, if the direction of the boss is to make the sales forecast regardless of how the goal is achieved, employees understand the message.

The other theory is rank has its privileges. This is not to suggest that senior employees do not receive a higher salary and various perks that are not available to lower-level employees, rather there are two sets of rules. There are strict rules for those near the bottom of the pyramid and a more laissez-faire attitude for those in senior positions. This is not a strong model for ethical compliance. This is often interpreted as "do as I say, not as I do." It is not uncommon for parents to set expectations for their children that they are unable to follow. For example, telling a six-year-old not to swear, while dad drops F-bombs in every conversation gives the child a message.

An ethical culture can be created by strong leadership. However, people who believe they are principled can be impacted by the dynamics of the workforce. Bad decisions can be made in an attempt to please the boss or go along with the group and some are unable to differentiate between the right course of action vs. what is best for the company. There is a common belief that doing what is best for the company is also best for the employee. In many cases, this is true, but it may be an unprincipled decision that may have future consequences.

A Formula for Ethical Behavior

There is a three-part formula that optimizes appropriate behavior and it can be very effective in ensuring compliance with rules and laws:

Step #1

Define the rule.

Step #2

> Have a process to identify those who do not
> follow the rules. Rule breakers should believe
> there is a realistic chance they will be caught

Step #3

> Ensure violations of the rules have
> consequences that are sufficiently severe
> that individuals will not want to incur a penalty
> for non-compliance.

Despite the simplicity of the formula, it can be difficult to implement and tends to be ineffective with the outliers in society. There are individuals who do not care about the consequences of breaking the rules due to amorality, desperation, intoxication or a mental disorder. For a multitude of reasons, there are people that just do not care about how their behavior impacts others. Most individuals make a rational decision based on the situation encountered. They tend to do the right thing since it is consistent with their personal values or a desire to avoid negative consequences.

Although as a society we pay lip service to the need for rules and consequences, we are often unprepared to play hardball and walk the walk. Consider motorists that are driving on a busy highway and the posted speed limit is 80 miles per hour. Most drivers are at least ten miles over the speed limit since they believe the posted speed sign is a suggestion rather than a rule. There is an assumption that if they do not exceed the speed limit by an excessive amount, there will be no consequences. If a motorist is driving exactly the speed limit, he may frustrate other drivers for not staying with the flow of traffic. In many cases, drivers who are in strict compliance with the law are the recipients of cursing, the finger and other forms of road rage. People are quick to understand the difference between a rule with consequences and suggested behavior. If the police set up radar traps and ticketed every motorist driving one mile per hour over the speed limit, the number of vehicles driving over the speed limit would be drastically reduced.

Politicians stress the importance of appropriate behavior and often operate under various ethical guidelines. The problem is that when there is a breach of ethics, the penance is slightly short of nothing. Perhaps they are censured or cautioned the action was inconsistent with their ethical standards. In other words, seldom is there a severe penalty. Something as simple as being kicked out of office, losing their pension or serving time in jail would be more effective than the gentle slap on the wrist and a promise from the offender to never do it again.

Consider the example of an individual who steals from her employer. If she is caught stealing, the employer's options include ignoring the theft, give the employee a warning, fire the individual or the consequences will depend on who is involved. If the thief is a high performer or related to an important person, it may be overlooked or followed up with a warning. However, if the employee has significant job performance problems, a termination may result. In many companies, management wants the discretion to take the action they believe appropriate in the circumstances, rather than standing on principle.

This raises the question - how much does a person have to steal before he or she is considered a thief? Let's be clear; we are discussing situations when employees knew what they are doing and took property belonging to the employer for their own benefit. This does not include honest mistakes, not following procedures or careless bookkeeping. If the employer's policy is to fire the employee regardless of the amount or individual involved and contact the police, there will a positive impact on the culture of the company. Many understand the motivation not to fire a thief, as perhaps the person has suffered enough and involving the police is just overkill. From a practical perspective, if employees understand the police will be involved, they may be less likely to commit a theft or file a wrongful dismissal suit against the employer if they are fired. If individuals were caught the first time they committed a crime, they might be the unluckiest criminals in the country. In other words, few criminals are caught committing their first offense, so it is reasonable to assume the theft or similar acts have been going on for a period of time. If the employer does not put a blemish on the thief's record, the individual will get a job elsewhere and may very well steal again. The subsequent thefts may never have occurred if the original employer had done the right thing.

Punishments for breaking the rules have to be consistent with the norms of society. For example, capital punishment has been eliminated or restricted in many jurisdictions despite evidence that it is effective in preventing repeat offenders from killing again. Some countries have cut off the arm of thieves, which creates a problem for their third theft. Despite the effectiveness of the punishment, it is considered barbaric by Western culture. If we wanted to reduce the number of traffic deaths, we could require occupants of vehicles to wear helmets. This would introduce a term that may be new to many women; it is called helmet hair. This legislation could save lives, but it is not consistent with society's norms. If we want to reduce distracting driving due to cell phones and other electronic media, a simple piece of legislation will address this issue. Anyone caught using their cell phone when driving, other than certain hands-free technologies, would have the phone confiscated by the police for sixty days. This would create too much public outcry so we can give them a $300 ticket instead, despite the potential to save tens of thousands of lives each year.

Building a Moral Compass

In addition to possessing specific skills, employers want to hire people, who are honest, have strong character and show leadership potential. Character can be as important as skill since talent can get an individual to a senior position, but a lack of character often makes it a short stay at the top. It is intuitive that opportunities will be denied to criminals, the dishonest and those that possess a poor work ethic. However, there is no litmus test to determine who possesses these traits. Prospective employers can take steps to filter out individuals with character issues such as checking references, police checks, or psychological tests. Even those lacking a moral compass will claim that they are honest and can always be trusted. Low character, but high charismatic individuals have a history of convincing others of their trustworthiness. In a post-truth society, men and women of strong character should have a distinct advantage. Values are not about saying the words; rather it is about living a life that is consistent with the principles of integrity and character.

Character is about choices and on a simplistic level it would make sense that one's character could be improved by making better choices, but the reality is those that make poor decisions continue to repeat the process. They focus on what is best for them in the short term, rather than determining the right course of action. It is easy to make the right decision if there are no negative consequences. Character is shown when there are negative ramifications for doing the right thing and the individual is prepared to suffer those consequences. This falls into the category of no good deed goes unpunished. Age, experience and maturity may allow character to develop in some people, while others are born bad and stay that way. Character is built through a complex interaction of parenting, friends, teachers and possibly religious institutions. A child that is able to model the appropriate behavior of loving parents has an incredible head start in character development. Society has a way of filtering out ethically challenged individuals. However, scoundrels are often able to game the system and have become leaders in politics, business and the church. Ethics is about doing the right thing, but it is a part of human nature to look out for number one and all too often we assume that the world does not see our "me first" attitude.

There is a strong correlation between success in the workforce and ethical behavior. As parents, managers and friends we often have an opportunity to influence the development of a moral compass in others. Perhaps the most important factor for building an ethical foundation is utilizing a principle known as falling your sword. It means that when a mistake is made admit the error quickly and unconditionally. It is the opposite of "it's not my fault because." Taking responsibility for mistakes and not making excuses that everyone can see through is an effective strategy. Although it seems counterintuitive, it is amazing that admitting a screw-up earns respect from one's peers and co-workers. If mistakes are accepted graciously, it encourages honesty and trust within the group. A byproduct of admitting mistakes is that there is no need to cover up the errors, which often results in additional consequences when the mistake is uncovered. This strategy is effective in the workforce and quite often when interacting with the police. An officer has incredible discretion how to handle situations that they encounter. It is easier to be emphatic or give someone a break if they are being honest and admit their culpability. There is an old saying in policing that you cannot talk your way out of a traffic ticket but you can talk yourself into one.

Ethical behavior is an important characteristic of successful people, but it very difficult for most adults to become more ethical and change the way they behave. Is it possible to raise the bar on our own level of integrity? We are imperfect creatures and most people have a dark side that we hide from the world. It is common to overlook our flaws and believe we are basically good people. We rationalize our bad actions and believe we can project an image of honesty to those around us. All too often we perceive ourselves as a hero who would certainly do the right thing if called upon. We understand that if we were present when Kitty Genovese was attacked, we would have been a stand-up person and called the police. In 1964, Kitty was returning from work at 3:00 am in the morning when

151

she was attacked with a knife, raped and died at the scene. Reports indicated that she fought back and screamed during the attack. According to press reports, thirty-seven witnesses heard the attack and did not call the police. Everybody who was not there believed they would have done the right thing. It is easy to be a hero in our mind, but in reality, doing the right thing is not easy as we may suffer negative consequences or not obtain something we wanted if we just used a small dose of larceny.

Bottom Line - Parents, executives and government leaders can create an ethical environment that will increase the probability of appropriate behavior. However, they must also set an example, so everyone understands that ethical behavior is one of their core values and non-compliance will not be tolerated.

Why do good people who enter the world of business and politics behave in an unethical manner? It tends to be the nature of the system they are entering, since standing on principle, rather than going with the flow, tends to result in a short career.

CHAPTER NINETEEN

WHEN FRIENDS STEAL AND CHEAT

The strength of the family is its individual members.
The strength of the individual is the family.

Many decisions are motivated by self-interest and looking out for "number one," but there is a higher standard that results in many individuals of strong character setting aside their personal ethics. To many of us, there is no greater priority than protecting our family, even at the cost of our safety or personal values. Family includes blood relatives and others who perform similar functions and are considered to be brothers and sisters. This would include:

- members of a union
- police officers
- soldiers in the same military unit
- gangs
- athletes

While driving home at dusk, a couple observes some teenagers breaking into a neighbor's house. It is known the family is on vacation for the next ten days. A common reaction would be to call the police, but panic sets in once the realization is made that one of the culprits is their son. Do they call the police and report the incident or is the decision made to handle it as a family matter without the involvement of the authorities? It is a dilemma for individuals when a family member commits some type of ethical or legal indiscretion as their sense of justice must compete with the need to protect their family. It is not uncommon for a family to cover for each other. Being at home with my spouse may be the weakest alibi provided to the police.

In its simplest terms, ethical behavior is just doing the right thing. The dilemma arises when an individual's core beliefs are in conflict. Individuals may want to do the right thing, but an overriding principle would be to take whatever steps are best for their family. Assume there is a bitter strike at ABC Widget Company which is located in a small town in Minnesota. Due to some picket line violence, the labor dispute has received national attention. If union members from across the country were surveyed and asked whether they supported union or management in this dispute, would it be surprising if more than 95% of the members supported their union brothers and sisters? It may not be relevant to their decision as to what caused the strike or if either side is being unreasonable. Solidarity is a key to union strength and in the vast majority of situations, they will support their union brothers regardless of the issues.

A military unit is in combat overseas. After a number of firefights, the unit is ambushed and one soldier in the fog of war mistakenly shoots an innocent civilian. Does the unit commander report it as negligence causing death? Would it be surprising if the unit stuck together and either did not report the incident or told a narrative that placed no blame on the soldier who fired the fatal shot?

A police department in Mississippi has advised their officers to have zero tolerance for domestic abuse. The abuser must be arrested. Two young officers arrive at a home after the wife called 911 and claimed she was assaulted by her spouse. The wife appears to have a black eye and possibly a broken nose. When they interview the husband, who is sitting in his car, he shows his detective's badge from a nearby county. Is the detective arrested per the zero-tolerance policy or is the fellow officer given a professional courtesy and not charged?

Two members of a gang are in a bar, and one gets drunk and punches a person at the next table for no apparent reason. The police are called and during their investigation, they interview the other gang member who was at the table at the time of the incident but did not take part in the assault. His possible responses to the officers include:

- My friend started the fight and he was not provoked by the injured bar patron. This is known as the truth.
- When the fight started, I was talking to a girl at the time and did not see the incident.
- The victim started the fight and my friend was only acting in self-defense.

We cannot be certain which option the gang member will select, but it will be a cold day in hell before he selects the first option. He will defend his brother, regardless of any personal consequences. Another way to look at the scenario is the option that could result in the worst possible consequences for the gang member who was not involved in the assault would be telling the truth.

Consider the case of a hockey player who has trouble putting the puck in the net, but his pugilistic skills were second to none. His team has the league's star player who goes by the nickname Bobby Hockey. In a recent game, a brutish defenceman dropped his shoulder and flattened Bobby Hockey. Our rough and tough hockey player knew his role on the team so later in the game he dropped his gloves, attacked the defenceman and lays a beating on the opponent. Our young hero knows his role; nobody touches our star. This is a relationship much like Wayne Gretzky and Dave Semenko in the heyday of the Edmonton Oilers. The player receives a game misconduct

155

but leaves the ice to a standing ovation. He knows his role and does it well.

At the end of the season our combatant is traded to a new team and in the third game of the season, he plays his former team led by scoring star Bobby Hockey. Early in the second period, Bobby brings the puck over the blue line and our pugilistic hero drops his shoulder and knocks the scoring star to the ice. He is unconscious and suffered a severe concussion. Our hero is kicked out of the game, but he knows he has done his job and would do absolutely anything for his new team. Bobby used to be a brother and teammate, but one is not necessarily in the same family for life.

Bottom Line – Protecting our family is human nature. Few would argue that Jean Valjean stealing a loaf of bread to feed a starving family member was not the right course of action. The desire to protect the family, either by blood or relationship, may be stronger than the need for self-preservation.

CHAPTER TWENTY

INSTITUTIONAL CORRUPTION

It does not take many words to speak the truth.

       Institutional corruption refers to situations when the reputation of the organization is considered more important than any abuse suffered by a victim. Our focus is not on the perpetrator of the crimes, but rather a bureaucracy that is able to throw the victim under the bus, without putting themselves in legal jeopardy.

       Although most priests are role models for their community, there is small human contaminate that corrupt our children. It could be .05% or 13%, as there is no way of knowing the exact number. This ranks among the greatest sins ever committed. When it appeared the situation could not get worse, we learned that the Church was involved in institutional corruption related to pedophilia once they became aware of the issue. Priests that were identified as pedophiles were transferred to other parishes in hopes the problem would go away. Not only did it not go away, but children in the new community were subjected to horrific acts. There were attempts to bury the problem in order to save the reputation of the church, even as more children were put at risk. Another tactic was to purchase the silence of the victims and include a confidentiality agreement that would not allow any talk of the abuse or details of the settlement. In many cases, the offending fathers were sent somewhere out of the public eye so they could reflect upon their transgressions. When rumors of the abuse started to spread, church officials were not running to the police to report this activity. Although it is difficult for the public to agree on any issue, most would agree that the proper action is to charge every priest who molested children and every church official who was involved in the cover-up. Most of us have not received the moral or ethical training of the clergy, yet we understand you do not screw children.

The institutional corruption that attempted to cover up the scandal has been a body blow from which the church may never recover. Priests sinned, leaders in the church tried to cover it up, but does the church have any culpability prior to the child abuse occurring? If an institution only recruited men that agreed never to have a normal sexual relationship with a woman, is it surprising that it would attract more deviants than other occupations? Perhaps if the church allowed female priests, this old boys' network would never have been allowed to attempt one of the greatest cover-ups in history. Not allowing women to be priests is a government-sanctioned exception to the diversity rules.

Consider the case of a party at large university where booze and pot are plentiful and students are in a partying mood. At 2:00 am a young lady passes out in a bedroom, only to awaken a few minutes later with a large man forcing her to have sex. She did not co-operate, she screamed and tried to fight, but the rapist carried on. When the ordeal was over, she returned to her dorm and told her roommate who called campus security. In the morning, she had a meeting with the university administration. They pointed out that she passed out from excessive drinking, was flirting on the dance floor and was dressed provocatively. What they did not mention was the rapist was the star of the university football team and was hoping to be drafted into the NFL. They convinced the young lady not to contact the city police and it would be handled internally, whatever that meant. Charges were never filed, the rape victim was thrown under the bus and as karma tends to work out, the football player was never drafted due to ongoing brushes with the law. The university prioritized its reputation and football program more than a rape victim. Justice would have been better served if both the rapist and university official spent ten years in prison. How many coaches at all levels have made the problems of star athletes disappear to protect their program and the athlete? How many victims never received justice?

How many daughters have joined the military and were raped by other soldiers and the crime was covered up? For a multitude of reasons, the military has buried many such cases. If the law gave the same punishment to the officer who ensured the soldier was not held accountable as the rapist, the motivation for such institutional corruption would be significantly reduced. Does a young woman have a greater chance of being raped if she enters a biker bar alone while dressed provocatively and gets drunk or joins the military? We cannot be certain of the answer, which is incredibly sad.

Institutional corruption also had a foothold in the corporate world and examples would include:

- A company buried hazardous materials in the 1960s when there were no rules concerning such disposals. The company has been requested by the government to acknowledge such disposals prior to the law being enacted, but the company denied all knowledge of any such issues.
- A sales rep is cheating on expense reports and stealing property for personal use. No action is taken since he is a high performer and any negative publicity may hurt the reputation of the company.
- The tobacco industry was aware of the impact of smoking, yet they continued to take the position their products were safe.
- Enron cooked the books and Volkswagen ensured their car emissions were not accurately

measured. In the case of Enron, Jeffrey Skilling went to jail, but he was an exception, rather than a rule for a white-collar criminal.

In all of these cases, the abuse was well known, but employees chose what was best for the company rather than standing on principle.

One would hope the medical community would not be involved in institutional corruptions, but such is not the case. Pharmaceutical companies are able to perform research in ways that the results are not reported to the appropriate authorities. Perhaps the most extreme example is the "Tuskegee Study of Untreated Syphilis in the Negro Male" which was run by the United States Health Services between 1932 and 1972. They studied the effect of syphilis on the human body. When it was determined that penicillin could cure this disease, the men were not given the drug. Many died yet no government official was charged.

Any group with a large number of members will contain a small group that consists of the worst of the worst. What if we are to take these people out of positions of authority? If all corrupt judges, teachers, policemen, priests, soldiers and politicians were relieved of duty, imagine the damage that could be eliminated. However, each group that contains these corrupt officials often has an association or superiors that protect its members.

Bottom Line - It is reasonable that officials in organizations will attempt to protect the reputation of the institutions that they serve. However, when these individuals suppress the commission of a crime in an attempt to protect their employer, should it be a criminal offense with harsh penalties? The deck is stacked against successful prosecutions as these institutions are rich, powerful and politically connected.

CHAPTER TWENTY-ONE

FINANCIAL FRAUD

*Laws are like cobwebs, which catches small flies,
but let wasps and hornets break through.*
Jonathan Swift

Crimes against people and property are declining. Governments can impact the level of lawbreaking by focusing on factors such as the number of policemen, gun laws, severity of punishment and how the law is applied to the drug culture. Although these so-called blue-collar crimes are being reduced, the same cannot be said of white-collar crime. The laws that define these crimes have not kept pace with techniques that corporate scoundrels utilize to fleece the public. Many crimes go unreported and when there is a conviction, the penalty is often a fine, rather than a jail term. This results in a corporation paying a fine and the culprits often keep their jobs. In other words, the shareholders pay the price for the malfeasance of executives.

Our criminal code is well drafted in terms of crimes against people and property, but there is room for improvement in the area of white-collar crime. Originally white-collar crime referred to crimes by the wealthy, corporations and government officials, whereas blue-collar offenses were against people and property. A key distinction between the two classifications of crime is detection. When a blue-collar crime has been committed, it is obvious as there are murder victims, property missing or knife wounds. With white-collar crimes, it may be unclear if a crime has been committed, as it may never be detected or there is a debate whether the action was criminal.

Consider the case of a bank robbery. A man walks into the branch of a bank, declares he has a weapon and runs out the door with $5,000. In a matter of minutes, four police cruisers are on scene with their lights flashing. For the next few hours, there will be a complete and comprehensive review of the crime scene and an all-points bulletin issued for the suspect. Let's assume a different scenario. The bank auditor has just discovered the bank has been defrauded of $500,000. This is not a 911 call situation, but if the bank manager called the police, would anyone show up that day? Depending on the size of the municipality, the police may or may not have the resources to investigate the possible crime, so it may be referred to another police force. When the bank officials and the police finally meet, the first few hours may consist of attempting to convince the police there has been a crime. All police forces have the resources to investigate crimes against people or property, but white-collar crime is a different matter. National forces such as the FBI, RCMP, or Scotland Yard are well equipped to handle such investigations, as are police forces in larger cities.

There are four factors that impede attaining justice for the victims of white-collar crimes:

- Allocating sufficient police resources.
- Updating the law to include the latest scams to hurt the public.
- Dealing with criminals who are wealthy and connected.
- Insufficient penalties.

Allocating Sufficient Resources - The police understand the need for increased scrutiny of white-collar crime given the growth of online child pornography, cyber crimes, identity theft and frauds committed by financial institutions. The resourcing and staffing of police departments is an ongoing negotiation with government officials. However, the banking industry is often regulated by government officials, rather than law enforcement. The decision to involve the police may be a political, rather than a fact-based decision.

Updating the Law and Regulations - Governments at all levels continue to pass laws and the legislation contains penalties for various infractions. Although the penalties outlined in the legislation may call for the possibility of fines and imprisonment, the reality is that white-collar crime cases that are prosecuted rarely result in time behind bars. If these cases were handled by the FBI and convictions resulted in the imprisonment of executives, financial fraud would be reduced.

It is a challenge to keep the legislation up to date with the latest and greatest ways to fleece the public. Given the vagueness of the laws and the multitude of employees that may be involved in corporate white-collar crime, governments have tended to pursue fines as the appropriate punishment. Companies can calculate the potential profits from breaking the law and weigh that against the probability of getting caught and any potential penalties that may follow. This calculation would often have input from the company's legal and finance departments and would be considered a standard risk analysis. Add the threat of jail time to the equation and the risk may no longer be worth the benefits. A perp walk and jail time may be the incentive some of these alpha males need to clean up their act. White-collar crime has traditionally been a male-dominated area, but as females attain more positions of power within the financial world, they will have an opportunity to smash another glass ceiling.

Wealthy and Connected Criminals - Many white-collar criminals are wealthy and this makes it more challenging to obtain convictions. They hire top-shelf legal representation and a plea deal may not be considered. Trials are lengthy, complex and convictions are not necessarily the outcome, even for guilty parties. In many cases, the financial frauds are carried on by large, powerful corporations who are politically connected. Justice in such cases should not be assumed.

Insufficient Penalties - What is often missing are severe consequences for white-collar criminals. When an organization commits a fraud, companies can be fined and conceptually, the executives could receive a prison sentence. Based on the shenanigans arising from the 2008 financial crisis, financial institutions were fined, but executives did not go to jail. When the company pays the fine, the shareholders pay the price, not the executive. If a criminal steals $5,000 during a bank robbery, he will almost certainly face jail time. If a financial institution commits a billion-dollar fraud, the expectation is the CEO walks and the shareholders pay.

Why do white-collar criminals who defraud clients of millions of dollars seldom go to jail, while a young man from a poor family can go to prison for stealing a few hundred dollars? White-collar criminals are nonviolent, often have no criminal records and are described by their lawyers as pillars of the community. Being white and rich probably works in their favor. One of the penalties they may levy is to participate in some type of community service. There was a famous rock star who was convicted of drug possession and was required to pick up the garbage in Central Park. This makes one wonder how the city employees who were paid to pick up garbage in the park felt?

If everyone the police arrested went to trial, the courts would be clogged. However, plea deals, stupid defendants and trials that can be finished a couple of days tend to expedite justice. However, in the case of many white-collar crimes, the trials are long and complex. Informing the jury and keeping them awake can be a challenge. If the fraudster is convicted, since he may have no prior criminal record nor a history of violence, the penalty may be a fine or community service. Some prosecutors may ask - why bother?

Case Study of a White-Collar Crime

A senior employee devised an ingenious fraud. He was able to convert inventory to his personal use and resell the products. The planning was ingenious and included falsified computer records, forgeries and unauthorized credits. To add to the complexity, he was sleeping with a co-worker who was in a position to catch the fraud. Although it may have been more luck than planning, the head office was in City A; the inventory was located in City B, while the employee sold the product in a different state. Once the company became aware of the fraud and quantified the loss, they approached the police in City A. The police reviewed the facts and claimed they had no jurisdiction. The company approached the authorities in City B who claimed they did not have jurisdiction. Once the out of state authorities was contacted, they agree they had jurisdiction, but they lacked the qualified staff to conduct a complex computer fraud investigation.

Not to be deterred, the company hired professional accountants to investigate the crime and turned the results over to the local authorities. The police agreed a crime had been committed, so the file was transferred to the Justice Department. After their review, they decided that although a crime had been committed, they would not proceed to trial.

On first blush, it made little sense that they refused to prosecute despite the fact they had the necessary evidence. Look at the facts from prosecution's perspective. The trial would be long and complex. It would be confusing for the jury to appreciate the complexities of computer fraud. The trial was expected to last two months and let's assume the jury stayed awake and found the defendant guilty, what sentence would the judge impose? Since the fraudster was a white-collar worker with no criminal record, the penalty may include restitution, community service, but probably no jail time. They were overworked, had a heavy caseload and did believe it would be prudent to bring this case to trial.

Banking and Investment Fraud

Financial fraud can result in families losing their savings, homes and retirement funds. Chasing these scoundrels is complex because they use corporations to conceal the transactions, enforcement is expensive and the penalties are inadequate. On the assumption you are not a Nigerian prince who needs help getting the family fortune out of the country, where is the top place to pull financial frauds? Sadly, Canada's financial rules and enforcement are a world-class flop. The scoundrels seldom get caught and the monies that have been defrauded may never be recovered. Canada lacks a national regulatory body, such as the Securities and Exchange Commission and they lack the ability to pierce the corporate veil that fraudsters hide behind. The politicians cannot get their act together and working families suffer. Perhaps the only good news is that the Canadian Prime Minister may offer a tearful apology for your loss – and little else.

Did you ever wonder why the Nigerian prince scam that has been around for decades never changes? By claiming to be a Nigerian prince, it eliminates smart people and leaves the unsophisticated to be scammed.

Connections and the Law

Perhaps the most astute observations on laws and ethics were made by Pierre and Justin Trudeau. Both men served as Prime Ministers of Canada and were charismatic and took leadership on many social issues. The ability to balance a budget or control spending were not skills they were able to master. Pierre became Prime Minister in 1968 and when questioned on the country's marijuana laws, he replied that people had the choice whether or not to follow the laws. However, they must be prepared to suffer the consequences if they are caught.

His son Justin became Prime Minister in 2015 and candidly shared the story of his brother's experience with marijuana and the law. In 1998, Justin's brother Michel was

166

involved in a traffic accident and the responding officers found a number of joints in his vehicle. As a result, he was charged with possession of marijuana. Former Prime Minister Pierre Trudeau used his connections and his son never had a criminal record. This reinforces the belief there are different rules depending on your status. One set is for the rich and well-connected; another for the middle class and unfortunately there may be a third set for the underprivileged and disadvantaged. This is unfair and unlikely to change. The ability to access proper legal representation can be the key to obtaining justice.

Bottom Line - White-collar criminals will find new ways to game the system and working families will continue to suffer. Eliminating investment fraud that can devastate a family's retirement should become a priority for our government. Putting these criminals in prison should become the norm, regardless of the scoundrel's lack of a criminal record and their lawyer's arguments concerning their standing in the community. Is hell empty as all the dark angels are working on Wall Street? It is important that financial institutions and their clients are not allowed to become a world of carnies and marks.

PART SIX

A BLEAK FUTURE FOR MANY FAMILIES

CHAPTER TWENTY-TWO

SNOWFLAKES, HARD-ASSES
AND NO SOLUTIONS

*If you are not a liberal at the age of twenty,
you have no heart. If you are not a conservative
at the age of forty, you have no brain.*
Winston Churchill

You walk into a restaurant with your spouse and the only other guest is Bill Gates of Microsoft fame. Does it make you feel rich when you realize the average net worth of every patron in the restaurant is over 25 billion dollars? The information is clearly misleading and using arithmetic tools that we learned in school, such as mean, mode and median, the numbers could be expressed in a more meaningful manner. The median income may be $50,000.

It is important to examine the numbers behind government stats because they can be misleading. Consider the following examples:

- In 2016, the United States saw a reduction in life expectancy for the second year in a row. The opioid epidemic is blamed for this disturbing trend.

- Infant mortality is the number of deaths for tots under one year of age for every 1,000 live births. The rate in the United States is comparable to many third world countries, as there are approximately six deaths for every 1,000 births. Despite the quality of their health care, it is not in the top 50 countries in the world and trails such places as Cuba, Hungary and Slovenia.

- When the unemployment rate drops below 5%, there is a sense the economy is strong and jobs are available for those seeking employment. However, over 30% of working-age adults are no longer engaged in the workforce.

Let's examine these troubling stats. Life expectancy for upper-middle class and wealthy families is increasing as the opioid devastation is primarily hitting working-class families and members of the underclass. Life expectancies for the haves are improving while the have-nots see a different result. When the results of both groups are added together, we have a misleading number since these early deaths are primarily hitting one subset of society.

The infant mortality numbers are horrific for Alabama, Mississippi and various poor rural areas of the United States. When these numbers are excluded, the United States is among the world leaders in healthy births. Upper-income families are experiencing excellent results, whereas the poor are not receiving the necessary level of care. The areas that have high rates of infant mortality also have higher rates of death for mothers in childbirth. These same states and rural areas have rates of death comparable to many third world countries. Once these poor and rural areas are excluded from the national average, the survival rate is among the best in the world.

Weaknesses of the unemployment rate statistics include failing to differentiate part-time and full-time employment, minimum wage jobs are combined with higher paying jobs and it does not consider individuals who are no longer for work. A more revealing stat is the labor participation rate. It measures the ratio of individuals that are employed or looking for work as a percentage of the adult population. This rate indicates that approximately 1/3 of adults are not engaged in the labor market. Many have become discouraged and dropped out of the labor force, while others are unable to work and are on disability insurance. The reasons are numerous, but if approximately 1/3 of adults have dropped out of the job market, what chance do they have to fund their retirement, without relying on government assistance?

It is important to examine the numbers to understand that we have become a society of haves and have-nots with a middle class that is trying to hang on. Often when we average the numbers, the middle looks comfortable, but it masks the plight of low-income families. When John Edwards was running for President of the United States, he talked of two Americas, which in simplistic terms divides the world into haves and have-nots. Income inequality has advanced to the state that a significant portion of the population has no chance to survive in retirement without public assistance. The issues facing those at the bottom of the economic ladder are attaining a critical mass and averaging the numbers with upper income and wealthy families can paint a misleading portrait.

When we examine non-mortgage debt, those in lower-income brackets take greater advantage of credit card debt and the horrifically expensive payday loans. As they enter retirement with debt, minimal savings and a lack of private pension income, it is a struggle to stay above the poverty line.

It appears we have a bimodal world of haves and have-nots and when we average the numbers, the plight of those at the bottom of the income scale are not accurately articulated.

Approximately 10,000 people turn sixty-five each day in the United States and a significant portion of these seniors have no pensions and minimal savings. Their food, housing and health care will be provided by governments who will finance these expenditures by some combination of higher taxes or larger deficits. If we were able to publish statistics on the families that constitute the low-income minimal pension (LIMP) segment of society, rather than averaging them with the rest of the country, it would become more obvious to understand the challenges these families are facing. Measuring their plight would be a first step towards proposing solutions.

The following groups are headed toward retirement and their worlds will have little in common. The first category is almost certain to have a financially secure retirement, whereas the underclass has almost no chance. In between is a middle class who are hoping for the best but live on a slippery slope.

New Elite - From the ashes of the old economy has emerged a new elite - the upper-middle class. They should enjoy a financially secure retirement and can provide a tremendous head start for their children's journey through academia and into the workforce. A hundred years ago, a key predictor of a child's opportunity for success was the income of the parents. Fifty years ago, success was available regardless of one's background. Unfortunately, the pendulum has swung in the other direction and children from wealthy and upper-income families have regained the advantage. Their parents have professional jobs, great incomes and are flourishing when other parts of society are struggling. These children have a number of advantages including a strong gene pool (common talk about racehorses, but uncomfortable topic with humans), their parents value education and they may receive parental assistance for tuition and the purchase of a home.

Middle Class - This middle class has a chance at a secure retirement if they can maintain their jobs until they retire, are members of a pension plan or aggressively self-finance their retirement. They are one economic downturn away from being dependent on government pensions to help pay their bills. Many middle-class families will be able to supplement their retirement by accessing the equity in their home or the receipt of an inheritance from their parents.

Low-Income Minimal Pensions - Working families that live from one pay to the next will struggle to finance retirement while individuals who were not employed for a significant portion of their adult life, due to disability, lack of opportunities or disinterest in working will be totally dependent upon governments to fund their senior years.

Impact of Inequality

Income inequality will not only impact the ability of families to finance their retirement, but it will alter the fiber of society over the next few decades. Some of the groups impacted are:

Children - The social mobility that emerged after the Second World War is reversing. Baby boomers could grab the golden ring by attending university or being hired into a union job. The status of their parents did not play a major role in their success. In tomorrow's world, the children of the wealthy and the upper-middle class will have many advantages over those from lower-income families. When baby boomers came of age, their families were aspirational, whereas the mood has changed for many working families and they see their children's future with a sense of desperation in a world where fairness is diminishing.

Students - If the goal is to become a member of the new elite, a post-secondary education is the pathway to most high paying jobs. However, many of the liberal arts degrees and online courses can result in students not acquiring any skills valued by employers and incurring a significant level of debt from student loans. Competition for top positions will be incredibly intense and the advantage may go to those with more than one degree. It is no longer sufficient to have a higher education; rather they must have the right education.

Families without a Pension - They either self-fund retirement or will be dependent on government pensions. Economic turbulence will make it challenging for low-skilled workers to pay their bills and save for retirement.

Non-Working Adults - Those who have survived for a significant portion of their life on welfare, unemployment benefits, disability payments or off-book income will not receive large government pensions. Their senior years will be a struggle and government pensions will replace other forms of public assistance.

Retiring Baby Boomers - Unless there is a massive investment in retirement communities and nursing homes, there will be insufficient beds and our health care system will be stretched. Senior ghettos may be a part of our future.

Governments - A tsunami of retiring baby boomers is going to be incredibly expensive when the government has to pay many of their expenses. There will be some difficult policy decisions for those in power and many are going to be hurt. The middle class can expect higher taxes and larger deficits to pay for the generation that went before them.

Educational Institutions - We have incredible universities, community colleges and secondary schools, but our model of education has become outdated. It is based on the theory that education is acquired before entering the workforce. Although some degrees provide specific skills, the focus of

174

many schools is to teach general knowledge with the assumption employers will provide the necessary skills when the students eventually acquire a job. There must be two fundamental changes to the educational model from the last century. Education does not end upon graduation; rather it must be a lifelong learning process. Secondly, students need to enter the workforce with skills valued by employers. As a society, we must ensure our students graduate with a valuable degree and without carrying a stifling level of debt.

Solutions

We have a retirement crisis and a significant portion of our country will be unable to pay their bills and must rely on government support. Although many families are in a position to fund their retirement, a significant segment of our country is not so lucky and will need help. We need solutions, but if we look at our current political leaders, do they appear to be up to the task? They are not discussing the issues let alone proposing solutions. We are a polarized nation and we appear to be rejecting the founding spirit that made us great and we are returning to our tribal roots. The snowflake perspective tends to favor spending money we do not have without making the necessary difficult decisions, while the hardasses on the other end of the political spectrum are prepared to provide assistance if it does not raise taxes or increase the deficit. Ideology is being spouted along party lines while a catastrophe awaits us. This may be the biggest crisis our generation will face, yet an intelligent debate on the issue is missing in action.

Bottom Line - We understand the issues to be faced in retirement, but there is a lack of serious discussions as to how these concerns can be either resolved or mitigated. The current strategy of kicking the can down the road for the next government to resolve is going to bite us in the butts. The government may supplement a meager lifestyle for families entering retirement without pensions or savings, but it is unfortunate that the wealth and genius of the baby boomer's generation could not resolve these issues before they ride into the sunset.

CHAPTER TWENTY-THREE

2039 – A REVELATION

Following the path of least resistance tends to ensure our dreams will never be fulfilled.

John is an accountant and he has had a bad day. He met with a family friend who had just turned fifty and was concerned she was unable to afford retirement. John was sure his knowledge of tax and retirement issues could save the day, but he was shocked by the outcome. After a review of her situation, it became clear that she was in a bad place. Her income barely covered her monthly expenses; she had no savings, no pension and a ton of debt that was rolled over from one credit card to another. Short of a miracle, there was no solution to her issues and he was frustrated that he could not provide any assistance. As he laid in bed that evening, he was overcome by his fears about retirement, the cost of health care, global warming, nuclear war and his children's future.

As he drifted off to sleep, something magical happened. He went to bed and woke in the year 2039. The future was unlike anything he could have imagined and the most significant event was the new political order. Intense polarization resulted in The United States becoming ungovernable. There were too many rifts between too many groups. There was a world of liberals vs. conservatives, the haves vs. the have-nots, gun owners vs. those favoring gun control, the religious right vs. secular thinkers, plus divisive issues such as health care, race relations, abortion and sexual equality. Realizing they were a country divided beyond resolution by reasonable men and women, the Congress and Senate of the former United States passed the Dissolution of the Republic Act in 2026. Without civil war and only scattered violence, the land of the brave had come apart at the seams. The greatest nation on earth split into three separate countries that shared a defense alliance and little else. The new countries were:

Bi-Coastal America - This country includes all of the states that border on the Atlantic and Pacific oceans, plus the Canadian province of British Columbia. The country was composed of the so-called "blue states" that had strong ties to the former Democratic Party. It has become a bastion of liberal thought. The name Bi-Coastal America was selected because of their proximity to the ocean and the inclusiveness of all its citizens regardless of their sexual orientation. Although Alaska was geographically aligned with the new country, their core values had a more traditional philosophy and they chose to join the Land of Liberty.

Land of Liberty - This fiercely independent and proud nation believes that gun rights, a pro-business philosophy, Christian values and freedom from government oppression are the core principles on which their democracy was founded. It extends from Texas in the South to Montana in the North and includes the former Bible Belt states of Alabama, Louisiana, Arkansas and Mississippi. This country believes the phrase in "God we trust" should not be a motto, but a way of life.

Heartland America - Although it was once known as the rust belt of America, this blue-collar world has a work ethic and a belief in middle-class values that has become the core principle of this great nation.

From Wisconsin to Michigan in the North and Missouri to West Virginia in the South, the focus of the newly created nation was fair-paying jobs for all families. The Canadian province of Quebec applied for admission, but they were rejected.

In all three countries, baby boomers were in the final stages of life and the cost of their care has overwhelmed the governments. Spending on retirement communities, nursing homes and health care were among the most significant expenditures. The values and philosophies of the new countries resulted in differing approaches to the issue of too many seniors relying on government assistance.

Bi-Coastal America

Of the three new countries, Bi-Coastal America had a beautiful blend of oceans and warm weather which acted as a magnet for retired families. When combined with a high level of government spending to support a generous social safety net, this country became the ideal home for retired families from around the world. As a result of the services provided, it had the highest taxes and largest deficits of the "three sisters." This was the nickname for the countries that arose after the dissolution of the United States. Bi-Costal American had a legislative agenda that was unthinkable only decades earlier and included:

Universal Health Care - The new constitution of Bi-Coastal America made it clear that health care was a right of all citizens. They copied the system of Canada and Western European countries that provided health care at no direct cost to patients. However, the cost was enormous. It was financed by a national sales tax, plus an increase in personal and corporate taxes. The top personal rate was 61%, the national sales tax rate was 10% and there was an inheritance tax with a maximum rate of 33%. Although no one was denied health care, there were a number of consequences of the new system. Doctors became quasi-employees of the state and there were restrictions on the number of tests that could be run and the amount of fees paid to doctors. As a result, many doctors left the country and moved to one of the other sister countries. Waiting lists for operations were a major issue and hospital construction could not keep up with the demand.

Although free health care was the pride of this new country, it did create an immigration problem that added enormous costs to the system. The sick and the elderly from Heartland America and Land of Liberty flooded to Bi-Coastal America. These immigrants, often lower-income people who for generations had lived in the United States, migrated to take advantage of free health care. The high taxes were not an issue as most of the immigrants were low-income retirees. There was a backlash by the majority of Latino residents who resented the influx of white working families who did not make a significant contribution to the public purse.

Legalized Euthanasia – It is common to hear comments that we treat our pets better in their final days than the elderly. The end of life can be a painful and lonely experience and many seniors wish it would come to an end in a dignified and controlled environment.

Certain European countries allow doctor-assisted suicide and Bi-Coastal America not only agreed with the European model but decided to push the envelope. The framers of their constitution believed in the individual's right of self-determination. As a result, doctor-assisted suicide was legal throughout the country. Initially, individuals could apply for the end of life procedure if they were in mental or physical pain and there was no cure for the source of their ailment. As the right to end one's life became a societal norm, the government passed legislation that became known as the "75 and Out" law. Officially the legislation was based on individual choice, but some critics contend the motivation was to save on the costs of caring for the aged or perhaps it was based on the controversial view that no one over the age of seventy-five has ever made a significant contribution to mankind. Regardless of the rationale, they passed legislation that would pay a $50,000 bonus to any senior between the age of seventy-five and eighty-five if they would voluntarily agree to be euthanized. Even when the contract was signed, individuals could change their mind up until the very last second. This was surprisingly popular as many seniors were able to check out of a sad and lonely existence and provide a small legacy for their family. There were voices of protest, but the constitution was based on the rights of individuals to live or not live as they see fit.

Representative Legislature Act - The liberal-leaning Bi-Coastal Senate wanted to ensure all minorities were properly represented in government. As a result, all federal, state and municipal governments had to reflect the community they served. Elected positions had to be at least fifty percent female and minorities were guaranteed proportional representation. These percentages were adjusted in the second term to ensure sexual preference was recognized. The only group that was not given special status were seniors. Surprisingly one group that benefited from the legislation was white males who had become a minority group in this newly created country.

Gun Laws - Unhappy with the cryptic gun provisions contained in the Second Amendment of the Constitution of their former country, gun ownership was severely restricted. The first attempt at reform was to follow the counsel of politicians supported by the gun lobby. They instituted strict background checks and passed laws that restricted sales to criminals and the mentally unstable. Although this approach produced a modest reduction in the number of mass killings, it was still legal to purchase military-style assault weapons to be used for target practice. Unsatisfied with the bill of goods that the newly elected politicians had been sold, they realized the error of their approach. Criminals, crazies and psychopaths were purchasing their weapons from criminals, rather than regulated outlets, so background checks and waiting periods were ineffective. If criminals were not going to play fair, neither was the government. Automatic weapons were outlawed and firearms could only be possessed by licensed hunters and farmers. There were a number of unintended consequences of the new restrictions as there was extra capacity in emergency wards; suicide rates dropped while policing and teaching became safer occupations. Although these changes were seen as positives by the citizens of Bi-Coastal America, they were mocked by Heartland America and Land of Liberty as insignificant advantages gained by giving up the right to defend their family and overthrow the government should they become overly intrusive in the lives of their citizens. There was an exodus of gun-toting, God-fearing residents, as some things are more important than free health care.

Land of Liberty

This nation was founded on conservative principles, the rights of the individual and Christian values. It was a continuation of the American spirit that rose from the days of the wild west. The key legislation that defined this country included:

Balanced Budget Legislation - Except in times of war and depression, the books had to be balanced over a four-year cycle. Although it created a pro-business environment, spending on infrastructure and social services had to be restrained in order to maintain defense spending. Health care was a continuation of the system used in the former United States of America. Those covered by employer-paid insurance had excellent coverage. Waiting lists were almost non-existence because of the influx of doctors leaving Bi-Coastal America. The elderly and the poor had a base level of coverage, but deductibles were high and not all medical expenses were covered.

Business Support Law - In order to promote business, the government eliminated the corporate income tax and minimum wage. The plan was wildly successful for companies and wealthy families. Corporations flocked to the Land of Liberty and economic growth outpaced other countries in North America and Europe. There was a high level of inequality as many working families were trapped in low-paying jobs with few benefits.

Eradication of Crime Legislation - In most countries, the consequences of being convicted of a crime was some combination of incarceration, fine or community service. Despite the severity of the penalties, crime persisted. The Land of Liberty made the elimination of crime a major priority, so they enacted a fourth type of penalty - chemical castration using anaphrodisiac drugs. For example, selling fentanyl would be a jail term, plus a dose of the drugs that would impair sexual performance for the next three years. Introducing severe consequences for criminal activity, resulted in a significant reduction in the crime rate. Unfortunately, the female crime rate did not change after the new legislation was introduced.

Reducing Unwanted Pregnancies - As soon as the country was formed, abortion was immediately outlawed. Stealing an idea from Bi-Coastal America's government-funded euthanasia legislation, a plan was introduced to pay drug users and single mothers a bonus of $10,000 to undergo a voluntary tubal ligation. According to the sponsors of the legislation, the program achieved its goals.

Insurance Protection Legislation - The country was subjected to ongoing natural disasters that included forest fires, hurricanes, tornados and earthquakes under land that had utilized fracking to extract oil and natural gas. Even though the legislature had passed a resolution confirming these disasters were not the result of man-made global warming, the insurance industry was suffering significant financial losses due to massive payouts to policyholders.

As a result, legislation was passed that gave certain protections to the insurance industry. Companies were no longer required to provide insurance in high-risk areas. As a result, property owners in cities such as New Orleans could not obtain coverage. The law also extended to health insurance. Insurers were allowed to obtain genetic testing before providing medical or life insurance. This allowed the insurance companies to weed out high-risk individuals that may develop certain diseases at some point in the future. The insurance initiative was very profitable for the industry, but it resulted in a large number of uninsured families. However, this was the price to be paid to support an industry that employed hundreds of thousands of people.

War with Social Media Companies - In 2033, The Land of Liberty declared war on a number of social media companies. There were numerous issues of contention including fake news, individual privacy and control of the internet. Actions by the government included the imposition of new taxes, declaring the companies to be a monopoly and holding the executives in contempt of Congress. What chances do companies have when big brother takes direct aim at their business? Not only did they fight back, but they brought the government to its knees, without going to court or incurring significant expenses. They controlled big data and used it to their advantage. The social media companies made public every pornographic site visited by elected officials and it was a long list. Not only did politicians resign in record numbers, but few men wanted to step up to fill the void. Surprisingly, those on the far right of the political spectrum seemed to have more unusual tastes. The net result from the mass resignations was an influx of female candidates. The next few years became known as the period of enlightenment as the new leaders moved from entrenched dogma to real leadership. The first legislative initiatives of the new government was the extension of health care to all citizens; ten months of paid maternity leave for new mothers and the legalization of same-sex marriage. It seemed overnight; they entered the twenty-first century.

Heartland America

Back in their grandparents' day, this was manufacturing territory. The auto and steel industries provided well-paying jobs for working families. The first president of this country was a populist who wanted to return to the glory days. Prior to his impeachment, he embodied the characteristics that promoted populism throughout the world. He promised simple solutions to complex problems and utilized an autocratic approach to governing. It was unfortunate that like many politicians, his greatest skill was selling false hope to working families. He was determined to return Heartland America to its former status as a manufacturing superpower. In order to achieve this objective, they instituted an apprenticeship program that ensured high school graduates would master an important skill. They also imposed duties on imported goods to ensure they would be competitively priced with locally manufactured products. They refused to engage in free trade negotiations and built a modern-day fortress America.

These programs resulted in a number of manufacturing firms reestablishing a presence in the country, but the advanced state of robotics and artificial intelligence resulted in increased output but few jobs. Manufacturing was still important to the economy; it just did not require many workers.

The isolationist strategy was unsuccessful and they hoped to amalgamate with one of their neighbors, but they were rejected by both Land of Liberty and Bi-Coastal America. They then turned their attention to the possibility of joining Canada. Heartland America was second only to Germany in apprenticeship training. The President admired the Canadian French Immersion Program. English speaking children were placed in programs that were exclusively taught in French and produced a generation of students that were in high demand for customer service and civil service jobs. Discussions with Canada broke off and the country was languishing with high unemployment and large deficits.

How did the breakup of the United States impact seniors? There was a mass exodus of retirees to Bi-Coastal America to take advantage of free health care. Heartland America had a high level of unemployment and Land of Liberty's economic policies resulted in low-paying jobs that made saving for retirement impossible. Retirees made up over fifty percent of Bi-Coastal's population and senior ghettos became commonplace. Many large businesses and wealthy citizens relocated to Land of Liberty. They tried various fixes, but nothing worked. They cut health benefits for smokers and overweight citizens, but that neither changed behavior nor materially reduced health expenditures.

There was eventually a backlash against immigrants as too many poor people (mainly from white working families) were moving from Heartland America and Land of Liberty to take advantage of free health care and the various support services for seniors. As doctors and nurses moved to Land of Liberty to receive higher wages, the level of health care services dropped to almost third world standards. There was insufficient tax revenue and too many seniors wanting free services. It appeared the liberal dream was dead. Poverty moved to Bi-Coastal America, while growth and wealth settled in The Land of Liberty, but only for a small segment of the population.

The Revelation of John

John awoke from his nightmare and had a revelation. He foresaw a severe humanitarian crisis as baby boomers hit the final phase of retirement and our government does not have the skill set to resolve the issues. John mused that the government might be the new Whore of Babylon, but we do not appear to have seven trumpets to warn of the upcoming apocalypse as it relates to retirement.

He understood the perfect storm of events that will lead to the crisis. They include:

- A demographic spike of baby boomers has retired and the cost to care for this departing generation will be enormous. We require more beds, health care services and community support as an influx of seniors will overwhelm the system.

- A decline in defined benefit pension plans has resulted in more families having to self-fund retirement.

- Too many families live on a modest income and entered retirement with minimal savings, debt and a lack of pension income. Saving for retirement was never an option when the family's income was barely adequate to pay for the necessaries of life.

- A lack of financial literacy makes it a challenge for families attempting to manage their assets to fund a retirement that could last over twenty-five years.

- Robotics and technology eliminated many high-paying jobs and the workers that have been displaced were often unable to replace their former income.

- Governments have such a high level of accumulated debt; they lack the financial flexibility to fund potential solutions.

- Workers are being forced into early retirement which results in savings that were earmarked for retirement being used to fund the family's lifestyle.

- Advancements in science extended our lifespan. It resulted in families having a longer retirement to fund and increased the time many seniors spent in nursing homes. Increased longevity resulted in financial pressure on families and governments to pay the increased cost of their care.

- Governments became the primary source of income for many families, but the level of pension income provided was below the poverty line.

The low-income minimal pension segment of society faced their own apocalypse. Living in poverty, the rise of senior ghettos, rationing of health care and the warehousing of seniors as they await death will become the new normal. However, the educated and skilled were living a life of leisure in their final years. Income inequality was becoming more extreme and those that were unable to look after themselves were living the equivalent of a third world lifestyle.

John understood the issues and came to the conclusion that governments appear to be incapable of implementing solutions. Regardless of the government of the day, poverty among seniors is here to stay. A significant portion of our population will be totally dependent on the public purse for all of their expenses for the last twenty-five or thirty years of their life. He knew that solutions could have been possible - a vibrant and growing middle class, increased financial literacy, an educational model based on teaching job-related skills and continued migration of the working poor into higher paying jobs. Governments had to be part of the solution, but the level of polarization in society has restricted almost any chance of meaningful reform. It appeared political parties were focused on selling their brand, rather than finding solutions for working families.

John's revelation scared the hell out of him. We are facing a humanitarian crisis and our politicians are doing their best imitation of deer staring at headlights. As income inequality continues to grow will those at the bottom of the income scale accept their fate? Unless governments crank up their printing presses, they lack the financial resources to eliminate poverty and must focus on providing a subsistent living for many seniors. As a society, we have a chance to address the issues, but is there any doubt we are going to blow it?

EPILOGUE

Families that have accumulated sufficient assets will start to enjoy the sweet spot of retirement when they leave the workforce and it will end as their health starts to decline. It may be the greatest time of their life as the drama and stress of working and child-raising are in the rear-view mirror. Retirees that are fortunate to reach this apex have the money to do as they please. They have the freedom to travel, volunteer, spend time with friends or do absolutely nothing. Those who are experiencing this lifestyle worked hard and are enjoying the fruits of their labor.

Many baby boomers who achieved a level of financial success are relishing their lifestyle. Perhaps their accumulated wealth will allow their children to reach this plateau, but the pathway to the sweet spot is becoming an uphill journey. The realities of the new economy are creating multiple barriers to entry. Many middle-class families believe they have a legitimate chance to experience the golden age of retirement, but layoffs, forced early retirements, divorces and health issues make the future uncertain.

Unfortunately, many will never enter this little bit of heaven on earth because they lack the financial resources. It takes a large amount of capital to finance a retirement that may last thirty years and those with a company pension, or a well-paying job have the best odds of success.

Despite working hard all their life, a large segment of the population will not experience the good life in retirement. The lack of a pension and minimal savings will result in a lifestyle funded by the government. They may be headed to a poverty trap they do not deserve. Solutions are possible, but they will take many years and vast amounts of government spending to implement. Social mobility is the key and that requires affordable education and ensuring everyone entering the workforce will possess a valuable skill. Educational institutions will be resistant to change since the current model is working very well for the employees of our very fine schools.

Family Support

Baby boomers that have lived the good life are in an excellent position to help their children who are in the workforce but do not have a clear pathway to a financially secure retirement. Perhaps their children have modest paying jobs or are not members of a pension plan. Inheritances whether they are prepaid or after the parents die can act as a retirement lifeline. Baby boomers have amassed an incredible level of accumulated wealth and their beneficiaries may inherit sufficient funds to finance their retirement

Working families that are not the lucky sperm of successful boomers can also benefit from a strong family support network, even if significant inheritances are not part of their future. An individual whose only source of income is government pensions will live below the poverty line, but a strong family unit can mitigate this potentially dire situation. Multiple generations living in the same home, parents supporting their children's' education and providing financial support for the purchase of a first home can smooth an individual's financial journey through life. For many families, it will be a difficult journey, but it will be more challenging for those who do not have a plan and must make the journey by themselves.

Our future of extreme inequality reminds me of the Cloud Minders episode from Star Trek. The elite lived in castles in the sky, while those on the planet's surface worked in the mines which were filled with zenite gas. Captain Kirk saved the day and ended the inequality between the elites and the Troglyte miners. The level of poverty in retirement will become a humanitarian crisis over the next few decades and we do not have Captain Kirk, a white knight or a superhero to save the day.